The EXECUTION of
MAJOR ANDRE

The EXECUTION of MAJOR ANDRE

JOHN EVANGELIST WALSH

palgrave

for ST. MARTIN'S PRESS

THE EXECUTION OF MAJOR ANDRE
Copyright © John Evangelist Walsh, 2001.

First published 2001 by
PALGRAVE™
175 Fifth Avenue, New York, N.Y. 10010 and
Companies and representatives throughout the world.

PALGRAVE™ is the new global publishing imprint of
St. Martin's Press LLC Scholarly and Reference Division
and Palgrave Publishers Ltd (formerly Macmillan Press Ltd.)

ISBN 0-312-23889-4

Library of Congress Cataloging-in-Publication Data

Walsh, John Evangelist, 1927-
    The execution of Major Andre / John Evangelist Walsh.
        p. cm.
    Includes bibliographical references and index.
    ISBN 0-312-23889-4
    1. André, John, 1751–1780.   2. Spies—United States—Bibliography.   3. Great
Britain. Army—Biography.   4. André, John, 1751–1780—Trials, litigation,
etc.   5. André, John, 1751–1780—Death and burial.   6. New York (State)—
History—Revolution, 1775–1783—Secret service.   7. United States—History—
Revolution, 1775–1783—Secret service.   8. Espionage, British—United States—
History—18th century.   I. Title.

E280.A5 W35 2001
973.38'6'092—dc21
[B]   2001019449

First Palgrave edition: October 2001
10 9 8 7 6 5 4 3 2 1

Printed in the United States of America.

Frontispiece: *Major John Andre, Adjutant-general of the British Army in America, about age 25, several years before his execution.*

For my son

TIMOTHY

with gratitude for
his cheerful assistance
and especially his
unerring critical eye,
displayed so uniquely
in his own book,
The Dark Matter of Words

CONTENTS

The EXECUTION of MAJOR ANDRE

PROLOGUE: SOLDIER OR SPY?

On a hot, humid day at the beginning of August 1842, one of the regular Hudson River excursion boats left its pier in New York City and steamed at a leisurely pace upriver. At noon it made its first stop, at Piermont perched on the western shore, where a crowd of passengers alighted. Among them was a young woman, Lydia Maria Child, one of the day's more respected authors. With a companion she took a room at a small tourist hotel from where the two could make their planned sightseeing trips around the area.

"The noontide sun was scorching," she would later recall, "and our heads were dizzy with the motion of the boat; but these inconveniences, so irksome at the moment, are faintly traced on the tablet of memory."

What was quite definitely and deliberately traced on Mrs. Child's memory was her visit to the sites connected with the last days and death of the young British officer, Major John Andre, hanged for his part in the treason of Benedict Arnold. It was to see these sites and to write about Andre's last days that she had gone upriver in the first place.

A leisurely ride in a carriage that afternoon brought the ladies to the village of Tappan where a guide joined them. Soon they stood together in a hushed silence "on the lone field where Major Andre was executed" some sixty years before, and where for long he lay buried. Situated on a low hill, the field commanded a sweeping view of the countryside almost down to the river. "I gazed on the surrounding woods," wrote Mrs. Child afterwards, "and remembered that on this self-same spot the beautiful and accomplished young man walked back and forth a few minutes preceding his execution, taking an earnest farewell look at earth and sky."

Pointing down the hill to a small house about a half-mile away, the guide explained that it had served as General Washington's headquarters at the time. Mrs. Child's response was strangely annoyed. "I turned my back suddenly upon it. The last place on earth where I would wish to think of Washington is at the grave of Andre . . . From the first hour I read of the deed until the present day I never did, and never could, look upon it as otherwise than cool, deliberate murder."

Fervently she adds that she is certainly *not* among those crude, unfeeling people who glory in the young officer's capture and execution. "I would rather," she declares emphatically, "suffer his inglorious death than attain to such a state of mind."

Down from the hill in the village itself the women were taken to "a small stone building, used as a tavern," where they were shown into "the identical room" where Andre was held while awaiting trial. "With the exception of new plastering it remains the same as then. It is long, low, and narrow, and being without furniture or fireplace it still has rather a jail-like look. I was sorry for the new plastering, for I hoped to find some record of prison-thoughts cut in the walls." In one corner of the room were huddled two mournful-looking doves, "all alone in that silent apartment where Andre shed bitter tears over the miniature of his beloved. Alas for mated human hearts! This world is too often for them a pilgrimage of sorrow."

The day's outing wound up with a visit to an old Dutch farmhouse whose elderly occupant was reputed to have been an eyewitness to the fatal event, "and whose father often sold peaches to the unhappy prisoner." To the women's delight, the old man readily confirmed all the stories about Andre's "uncommon personal beauty," and they were equally pleased to have his "vivid remembrance of the pale, but calm heroism with which he met his untimely death."

Mrs. Child's account of her visit to Tappan appeared in her well-received book, *Letters From New York*, published in 1846. Her tone may now sound effusive and a bit strained, yet nothing of what she said about Andre or the visit would have struck her readers as out of the ordinary, not even the slur on Washington. By that time the affecting tale of the unlucky British major had become a staple of American history, familiar to all—how he'd been captured while on a secret mission to consult with the traitor Arnold, how he'd been tried and condemned as a spy even as he and others angrily denied the charge, how finally at the express order of Washington he'd been hanged, going to his death in a marvelous display of grace and courage.

Whether it had been right and just to call him a spy, whether he should have suffered death or been held as a prisoner of war, were questions hotly debated over and over in the century following the execution. Today, while less urgent, less agitated, the question still reverberates, still finds earnest advocates eager to take the negative. As recently as 1976 a respected scholar designated Andre's trial before a board of American generals as "a Star-Chamber proceeding," yielding a rigged verdict, also charging that Washington shamefully condemned the brave officer as a "scapegoat."

Integral to the old argument has always been Andre personally, with his impressive array of qualities and abilities that earned him the sincere admiration and warm regard of all who knew him even slightly, friend and foe. This part of the legend received its final impetus a dozen years after the Child book and from none other than Washington Irving. Published in 1859, Irving's five-volume *Life* of George Washington treats the Andre story sensitively and in greater detail than any writer before him. About Andre on a personal level he has much to say:

"The character, appearance, deportment, and fortunes of Andre had interested the feelings of the oldest and sternest soldiers around him, and completely captivated the sympathies of the younger ones. He was treated with the greatest respect and kindness throughout his confinement . . . Never has any man, suffering under like circumstances, awakened a more universal sympathy even among those of the country against which he practised. His story is one of the touching themes of the Revolution, and his name is still spoken of with kindness in the local traditions of the neighborhood where he was captured."

One of those younger soldiers who came under Andre's spell, adds Irving, was the twenty-five-year-old Alexander Hamilton, then serving as an aide to Washington. During Andre's ten-day imprisonment, Hamilton talked with him many times, officially and unofficially, and left a glowing description of what he saw and felt, a description given by Irving in paraphrase. Andre was a young man "well improved by education and travel, with an elegant turn of mind, and a taste for the fine arts. He had attained some proficiency in poetry, music, and painting. His sentiments were elevated, his elocution was fluent, his address easy, polite, and engaging, with a softness that conciliated affection, [and] a diffidence that induced you to give him credit for more than appeared." Actually Hamilton had specified "a peculiar elegance of mind and manners, and the advantage of a pleasing person," putting some emphasis on a fact noted by all and often remarked, that Andre was one of the handsomest men they'd ever seen.

No less impressed by Andre personally and by his brave sacrifice were his own people, a fact that Irving highlights by quoting from a letter written in London shortly after the execution: "The fate of this unfortunate young man [has] raised more compassion here than the loss of thousands in battle . . . Panegyrics of the gallant Andre are unbounded; they call him the English Mutius, and talk of erecting monuments to his memory." The word *gallant* was quickly tied to his name so that no one during the nineteenth century and until quite recently needed further identification than "the gallant Andre" to know who was in question.

Two years after Irving there appeared the first full-scale biography, and with that Andre's apotheosis was complete. Written by an American, Winthrop Sargent, whose ancestors fought in the Revolution— one was wounded at Bunker Hill—the book offered a detailed, highly favorable treatment of its subject's "Life and Career." A forty-page discussion takes up the controverted question of his final end, drawing on principles and examples from ancient military history and foreign nations. Yet the conclusion, strangely, is by no means clear. Rather timidly and hesitantly, the author himself declares for Andre's guilt, while leaving his readers floundering in a welter of argument and counter-argument. As with so many others, his final word, couched in the annoyingly elaborate tone of the time, manages to put the emphasis quite elsewhere:

> . . . when all is spoken, shall we pronounce Andre's an unhappy fate? Has not the great law of compensation gilded his name with a lustre that in life could never, with all his ardent longing for fame, have entered into his most sanguine hopes?
>
> If he perished by an ignominious means, he perished not ignominiously; if he died the death of a felon, it was with the tears, the regrets, the admiration of all that was worthy and good in the ranks alike of friend and foe.
>
> The heartiest enemies of his nation joined with its chiefs in sounding his praises and lamenting his lot . . . His motives, inimical as they were to our cause, were eminently respectable . . . He died in the morning of his life, before success had stained with envy the love that all who knew him bestowed upon his worth . . . His dust is laid with that of kings and heroes, and his memory,

Of every royal virtue stands possessed,
Still dear to all, the bravest and the best.

The years since Irving and Sargent wrote have brought little change in the public and indeed scholarly perception of the gripping story. Andre's "fate" is still sadly lamented while the "justice" of it is still argued, though perhaps not so frequently or with the same urgency felt in earlier times. Now the verdict generally tends to the position that Andre did indeed act the part of a spy, even if reluctantly, even if accidentally, and deserved to die. Yet for many, certainly for me, the fascination of the problem remains as strong as ever, especially remembering that Washington himself, by whose hand Andre went to the gallows, conceded the unusual nature of the case. "He was more unfortunate than criminal," wrote Washington later, "and as there was much in his character to interest, while we yielded to the necessity of rigor, we could not but lament it."

Equally relevant, though never made quite plain in all that has been written, is the implicit contradiction underlying the Andre story, for both sides but in particular the British. Early praised by his king and defended by English historians, in his homeland Andre was and is honored as a hero of the Revolution, despite the all-too-evident fact that, entirely on his own, he made a blundering failure of his supremely important mission. Few today will deny that British control of the Hudson at West Point, splitting the American forces in two and giving them mastery of a wide stretch of important territory, would have brought a prompt halt to the Revolution. With Benedict Arnold's startling offer to betray the West Point fortifications, where he commanded, the British had final victory in their grasp, and they knew it. That chance was lost *only* because of Andre's incredibly inept performance.

Conducted secretly at the highest levels of American and British military authority, where it was all but immune to discovery or interference, by all the rules of probability and common sense the plot to betray West Point *should* have succeeded. That it didn't was a fact that struck all at the time with astonishment, so much so that for many the only possible explanation involved the hand of God. "The interposition of Providence," Washington called it, using a phrase often echoed by others, then and since.

In America Andre is also fondly remembered and honored, here for his youthful grace and bravery, his loyal devotion to country, and on a deeper level for being in a real sense a symbol of the awful waste of war. So excellent and able a young man, deprived so suddenly of a life that promised much good, inevitably strikes a sensitive mind as unutterably tragic, exposing the essential barbarity and futility of armed conflict. The fact that this particular excellent young man had been intent on crushing all hope of independence for the struggling patriots—with the capture and possible killing of Washington himself included—made no difference in the kindly estimate of his worth. At his execution real tears were copiously shed, a heartfelt reaction repeated figuratively from time to time ever since.

The overlooked truth, I think, is not so pleasant as the legend will have it, in fact is infinitely more complex than that. For all his surface charm, amiability, and talent, young Andre, as I read the evidence, was a far more complicated man than has been suspected. Not at all the open, accommodating personality he seemed, he was as I see it one of the most calculating of individuals, keenly aware of his peculiar power to impress and fascinate. It was a lesson he learned and began practicing early in life, and is the true explanation for his rapid rise in the British military. A captain, he was promoted by General Sir Henry Clinton over many more senior officers to become, at age twenty-nine, Adjutant General of all British forces in America. I also see it as the reason why he, as a personality, became a main focus of the Arnold treason story, why the glare of the spotlight falls on *his* fate, *his* behavior, *his* sad doom, rather than where it should fall, on his truly epic failure in the enterprise.

Portrayed as a hero of grand proportions, moral as well as military,

Andre in reality was a starkly ambitious, cunningly self-willed ma-
nipulator, crudely arrogant beneath that pleasing exterior.

From the moment of his capture his every thought was of himself,
his least move designed for his own benefit without regard for how
it might affect his assigned mission or anyone or anything else. At
first his sole motivation was to save his life at any cost, a purpose he
disguised as a matter of gentlemanly honor, aristocratic pride, openly
confessed. When that hope began to glimmer he didn't despair but
calmly determined to control the perception of his last hours in order
to obliterate the embarrassing fact of his colossal failure. In this he
was eminently successful, down to the level of his actual captors,
three young American militiamen whose reputations he tried to de-
stroy by insinuating lies, and in good part succeeded.

Here, especially, the chilling truth about Andre's inward-looking
ego becomes evident. At every moment of his captivity to everyone
with whom he spoke, all who were allowed to see him, his every
separate action, even the smallest, was meant to add another stroke
of color to the flattering portrait of himself he was painting for posterity.

Most clearly can this be seen on the day of his execution, his last
five hours of life. From his rising out of bed at seven A.M., to the
deadly snap of the rope at noon, he quite deliberately and deftly acted
a part, every bit as calculated as his earlier moves in the gathering
drama. In truth it was an astonishing performance to deliver on such
an occasion, his ability on this final morning to play the string out
so unflinchingly. Truly it speaks for something extraordinary in him,
some submerged quality of spirit, which in itself deserves to be recorded and remembered.

The basically narrative form (of course strictly factual) in which
I've chosen to present all this—in contrast to the standard historical
approach of analytical exposition—gives a happy advantage. A continuous narrative certainly supplies a naturally dramatic setting for
events that cry out for dexterous handling. More importantly, it al-

lows a sharper, more evocative focus on what is still the central question, whether Andre is to be seen as a soldier doing his duty or as that despised thing, a spy (in his day spies were looked on as low, twisted creatures, their lying deception far beneath a gentleman's notice, and no military officer would willingly consent to serve as one).

Opening with an account of Andre's trial (more accurately a military hearing or court of inquiry), I present in detail the charges brought against him as they were laid out by the American prosecutor: using collateral documents I fill out the official account of the trial as published soon afterward. Then come the counterarguments of the British as played out in the context of the urgent, last-minute, flag-of-truce negotiations, followed by Washington's desperate attempt to work a behind-the-scenes trade of the spy for the traitor.

At this point we pause to look back in a continuous narrative covering the ten hectic days and nights of Andre's mission before his capture. With comment at a minimum, these four chapters give the separate events on which the charges were based, beginning with Andre's coming ashore from the British sloop for his midnight meeting with Arnold. Here are laid out all the necessary facts of the operation—making graphic such crucial matters as sequence, motive, and causation—allowing each reader to become his own judge.

A detailed, minute-by-minute recital of the condemned man's remarkable final day, based on the reports of eyewitnesses, brings Andre's affecting story to a close. Following that, I give a portrait of the three captors (the fullest to date, I may add), their subsequent lives, and the havoc caused to their good names and reputations by Andre's falsehoods. An Epilogue ties up a few loose ends, in my view of peculiar interest.

At times, in order to clarify and make more immediate some of the story's murkier parts, I use a reconstructive method which turns description into dialogue (*without* quotation marks, which as usual are reserved for direct citation of documents*). With so much con-voluted material to be handled, where the undoubted facts can be easily dug out I prefer the immediacy of a spoken exchange, of course faithfully mirroring the reality.

Perhaps I should add that this narrative-style method is not so very different from what may be termed standard historical writing. All it does is *separate* the two main strands that go to make up the more usual approach, that is, *fact* (definite or probable), and *the analysis of fact*. In my main text I arrange the first strand, the facts, in a continuous narrative that gives my own view of their meaning, ob-vious or latent. The second strand, analytical discussion of the facts and their sources, I transfer to the extensive section of Notes. Of course, not everyone will care to bother with these Notes. Herded as they are at the book's rear, they will molest no reader who chooses to avoid them.

Also apparent, I trust, is the fact that at *no* point in the recon-structed narrative do fictional or purely imaginative touches intrude. All depends on established documentary fact and sober inference from those facts.

Standing in the doorway of the old Mabie Tavern—the same building that held Andre a prisoner and which so moved Mrs. Child—I looked out along Tappan's short, narrow Main Street. A hundred yards away to my left was a small brick church sitting on the same plot of ground that in 1780 held the Old Dutch Church in which Andre had his trial. Out of sight a half-mile along a curving roadway to my right still stood Washington's old headquarters, the little De Windt house. I walked down the porch steps, turned left and went along the street fifty or so feet, then turned left again. Before me rose on a gradual slope the same road that Andre, to the

---

*To this rule I permit myself one partial and I believe allowable exception, the capture scene. See the Notes, 191–222.

sound of muffled drums rolling intermittently and the murmur of the watching crowds, walked to his death.

In the road's middle I trudged slowly up, trying to fit my mood to the sensations of a man walking to his death. I listened for the rolling drums, looked for the sorrowful faces along the way. Nothing. All I could hear was the wind in the treetops, the sound of my soles grinding the gravel underfoot. All I could see were the drifting clouds low overhead.

Near the top a narrower, tree-lined street opened on my left. I turned in and after a few minutes came to a dead end where sat a low, square block of granite inside an iron fence. One polished face was covered by engraved writing, beginning with, "Here died October 2, 1780, Major John Andre . . ." The body, I knew, had been buried on the spot in a grave dug beside the gallows. Years later the remains were exhumed and returned to England to be interred in Westminster Abbey. Andre fell "a Sacrifice to his Zeal for his King and Country," reads the inscription on the Abbey's ornate monument in a last subtle if excusable distortion.

Andre's zeal was not at all for king and country. It was for himself alone and at every step it led him wrong. That's the part of the story that has yet to be told.

PART ONE

I

THE PRISONER

A loud, clattering rumble, the distinctive sound of a cavalry troop on the move, woke the still air of little Tappan village, bringing heads expectantly erect and sending pedestrians scurrying to the roadside. Swinging at an easy canter into the short main street from the north, the troop slowed to a walk as the line of paired riders straightened out. Except for one man at the middle all wore the blue-and-buff uniform of American Light Dragoons. The man at the middle wore civilian clothes: plain nankeen knee-britches with boots, shirt, vest, and dark jacket, but no hat. Curiously, over his shoulders was thrown a blue American dragoon officer's cloak, giving him somewhat of a soldierly bearing. Though his wrists were bound tightly together in front of him he sat his mount comfortably.

Halfway along the main street the head of the troop came abreast of the Mabie Tavern, a long, low building of reddish-gray stone that served as the American army headquarters. With much shuffling of hooves it drew up and the officer in front dismounted, beckoning to two riders near the prisoner. They climbed down, helped the bound man off his horse and walked on either side of him up the tavern steps, following the officer. Greeting them at the door was General Nathaniel Greene, Commander of American forces in the area. A tall, sturdily built man, Greene for a moment stood looking curiously down at the shorter, slighter prisoner. What struck him mostly, as he wrote next day in a letter to his wife, was the man's "apparent cheerfulness," which in the circumstances seemed downright odd.

Saying nothing, Greene turned and led the way inside.

On the left were two rooms, front and back, which Greene was using as his office. On the right were two smaller rooms, also front and back, that had been assigned to the prisoner, a sitting room at the front with a bedroom behind it. In sending the prisoner to Tappan, General Washington had stipulated, "I would wish the room for Mr. Andre to be a decent one, and that he be treated with civility." But he took care to add that Andre must at all times be well guarded, two men always in the room with him in addition to those stationed outside the building, "to preclude the possibility of his escaping." He will certainly make the attempt, cautioned Washington, "if it shall seem practicable in the most distant degree."

With Andre, closely watched by two officers, locked in the sitting room, and with some thirty dismounted dragoons ringing the tavern, muskets at the ready, the other troopers moved off to their camp outside the village.

The commanding officer of the troop, twenty-six-year-old Major Benjamin Tallmadge, had been in charge of the prisoner almost from his capture six days before. Now, having delivered him to Tappan where the trial would take place, he was anxious to be relieved of his responsibility, and for that he must report personally to Washington, also on his way to Tappan. In fact, Tallmadge was told by an aide of Greene's, the Commander-in-Chief had already arrived. He could be found at the De Windt house.

Also converging on Tappan that day, September 28, 1780, was an impressive array of American generals, some dozen of them, all summoned by Washington to serve as judges. President of the Board, or court of inquiry, was Major General Greene himself, aged forty, the officer most respected by Washington (in fact already suggested by

Washington to Congress as his replacement if needed). Five other major-generals included William Alexander (Lord Stirling), who at age fifty-four was the court's oldest member. Youngest at a startling age twenty-three was the French nobleman, the Marquis de LaFayette (given his commission as a political move, it had worked out well, the "boy-general" proving to be a mature and able officer, as well as an important contact with France, then about to join the Americans in the war). The Prussian drill-master Baron von Steuben, Scottish-born Arthur St. Clair, a veteran of the French and Indian War, and Robert Howe, engineer and a British officer before the Revolution, completed the list.

Six judges, all major-generals, might seem an adequate number for evaluating evidence in a military trial, but for some reason Washington wanted more, a lot more. No fewer than eight brigadiers were also assigned to the case, ranging in age and experience from the thirty-year-old artillery expert Henry Knox, to New England's rough and ready John Stark, fifty-two. In between were the Marblehead sailor, John Glover, who had organized Washington's dramatic crossing of the Delaware for the attack on Trenton; James Clinton, long-time professional soldier and father of DeWitt Clinton; Irish-born Edward Hand, an officer in LaFayette's elite corps; Sam Parsons, Harvard graduate and a lawyer before the war; Jed Huntington, originally a merchant and also a Harvard graduate; and John Paterson, who at age thirty was the army's youngest brigadier.

All were officers of proven mettle and understanding of the fine points of military usage. At least it couldn't be said that the Commander-in-Chief was trying to control the outcome. Obviously, coordinating so many views and opinions greatly increased the possibility of disagreement.

Presenting the charges against the prisoner as informal prosecutor would be another young man, Colonel John Laurence, thirty, the army's Judge-Advocate. It was Laurence who visited Andre at the Mabie Tavern the day of his arrival to inform him of the planned proceedings. A straightforward court of inquiry was to be held, he explained, in effect a hearing convened at General Washington's direction. The Board of Generals, as instructed by the Commander, would examine all aspects of the affair and report their conclusions as to Andre's exact status, whether spy or not, and the proper punishment, if any. Washington at his own discretion, as provided by law, would make the final decision, accepting, rejecting, or refining the Board's verdict.

Probably Laurence did not bother explaining that Washington's private opinion was that no hearing was needed, that the known facts of the case justified, as he said later, "the most rigorous" summary judgment, immediate hanging. Why in that case he called for an inquiry he never said.

At the inquiry, Laurence added, Andre would be questioned by members of the Board as they wished. But he would be given every opportunity to make his defense, and it had been agreed that he would not be pressed to give the names of any who might have acted with him. He might consider writing out a statement to be read to the Board as the best means of assuring the completeness and coherence of his testimony. No witnesses were scheduled, though they could be readily called if required.

No length of time had been set for the hearing, finished Laurence, though from what he knew of the case he felt it might occupy as little as a day. Next morning at eight sharp they would begin, in the little Dutch church just down the road. They passed it on the way in, a square, one-story brick building topped by a stump of spire. Would Major Andre need more than an hour in the morning to prepare? Would a call at seven be soon enough?

A jaunty smile lit the youthfully handsome features. Colonel Laurence was very good to bring him the information, replied Andre pleasantly. Seven would do nicely.

AT THE DE WINDT HOUSE Major Tallmadge was ushered by an aide into Washington's office. Himself a six-footer, tall for the time, he

Tappan, New York (contemporary oil sketch). At right is the Dutch church in which Andre was tried. The Mabie Tavern is among the cluster of buildings to the left. Below: The Mabie Tavern at Tappan where Andre was held prisoner.

had to look up to meet the eyes of his imposing commander, four inches taller. The prisoner was safely delivered as ordered, reported Tallmadge, also explaining the security arrangements at the Mabie Tavern. On the way down, he added, they'd met the special troop of dragoons detailed to act as additional guards along the way. But the British hadn't tried anything and there'd been no incidents.

For nearly a week Washington had lived and worked within a few feet of where Andre was held but had yet to see or question him. Now he asked Tallmadge about the prisoner's condition. Was he still in good shape physically? Had he talked much on the way down from West Point? What sort of man was he? The questions were not posed out of mere curiosity, for Tallmadge was no stranger to his Chief. In addition to serving as Major of the Second Light Dragoon Regiment (Connecticut), at Washington's specific request he had frequently and in person conducted intelligence operations among the British forces on Long Island and in New York City. His views and opinions were very much valued by the Commander.

Yes, Andre had talked freely all the way, answered Tallmadge, and for days before that. He had proved to be a fairly garrulous man, at one point rattling on about British plans, if the Arnold plot had succeeded, for sending a large force against the deliberately weakened West Point forts. While the details of Tallmadge's replies to Washington's questions are lost, their substance can be read in two letters he wrote within days, largely relating to Andre personally.

In the first letter he confesses, "I never saw a man whose fate I foresaw whom I so sincerely pitied. He is a young fellow of the greatest accomplishment . . . He has unbosomed his heart to me so fully, & indeed let me know almost every motive of his actions since he came out on his late mission, that he has endeared me to him exceedingly." In the second he calls Andre "one of the most accomplished young gentlemen I ever was acquainted with. Such ease and affability of manners, polite and genteel deportment, added to a large understanding, made him the idol" of his superiors, fellow officers, and subordinates.

Here was praise indeed, especially coming from an enemy, but it wouldn't have surprised Washington. Already he'd heard similar sentiments openly expressed by the younger members of his own staff, including his aide, Colonel Hamilton, who'd been much in Andre's company. ("I wished myself possessed of Andre's accomplishments," confessed Hamilton in a letter to his fiancée, while to a friend he declared that "There was something singularly interesting in the character" of the man.)

Even with Tallmadge's glowing account added to those he'd heard from his own aides, Washington made no plans to meet the paragon and see for himself what all the fuss was about. The only sign he gave that the prisoner might be someone out of the ordinary was to have Andre's meals sent up from his private kitchen.

One relevant fact about Andre's background, not then or for years afterward known to the Americans, concerned his earlier military service. As aide-de-camp to General Charles Grey, the same "No-Flint" Grey so hated by the Americans for his needless barbarity, he took part in two notorious, well-documented massacres of American troops. In surprise night attacks at Paoli, Pennsylvania in September 1777 and a year later at Old Tappan, New Jersey, Americans who had surrendered or been captured were mercilessly put to the bayonet. At Paoli, as Andre approvingly states in a regimental diary kept by him, the British regiment "coming in upon the camp, rushed at them as they were collecting together and pursued them with a prodigious slaughter."

For the second massacre, that of Baylor's dragoons, who were surrounded while asleep in barns, the diary entry matter-of-factly notes that "The whole corps within six or eight men were killed or taken prisoner." Most of the dead, as investigation later established, were killed in the act of surrendering.

Though Andre didn't wield a bayonet, perhaps didn't actually order men killed, he was present and in action at both places, being later thanked by General Grey for his assistance "in the warmest terms," as Andre himself expressed it. Had Tallmadge, Hamilton, and

their fellow officers been aware of his link to these shameful incidents, their overflowing sympathy for the gentlemanly prisoner would
have been far less intense.

That evening, finishing his long day of travel and responsibility,
Tallmadge paid a last call on the man he'd been guarding for nearly
a week. As he entered the room, Andre greeted him with a cheery
smile, at the same time picking up the dragoon officer's cloak. Thank
you for the use of your cloak, Major, he said, adding, I confess I'd
have been positively ashamed coming to American headquarters
looking as drab as I do in these ill-fitting civilian things.

Accepting the garment, in a friendly tone the smiling Tallmadge
replied that he was glad to be of service. Apparently it never struck
him that his captive, in wearing the stylish, high-collared cloak, had
managed to make his entrance in the American camp not as a lowly
spy but with a decidedly military air.

II

IN THE COURTROOM

A narrow splash of dark blue and burnished gold ran across the open space at the front of the Old Dutch Church, the epauletted uniforms of fourteen generals seated behind a random assortment of tables strung in a line.

As all sat silent, a door at the side of the room opened and Major Tallmadge entered, followed by a half-dozen armed guards ringing the bright-faced Andre. He was taken to a small table and chair facing the center of the line of judges where he paused, made a slight bow of acknowledgement to General Greene seated at the line's center, then sat down. From his breast pocket he drew a folded sheet of paper which he smoothed out on the table before him.

Colonel Laurence? invited General Greene, nodding at the prosecutor to begin. The Judge-Advocate rose to his feet at another table, set between Andre and the judges and off a little to one side.

Your Excellencies, said Laurence, rising and bowing slightly, I have here an order from General Washington dated this morning, September 29, 1780. Picking up a small piece of paper, he read it out:

Gentlemen: Major Andre, Adjutant-General to the British army, will be brought before you for your examination. He came within our lines in the night, on an interview with Major-General Arnold, and in an assumed character, and was taken within our lines in a disguised habit, with a pass under a feigned name, and with the enclosed papers upon him.

After a careful examination you will be pleased, as speedily as possible, to report a precise state of his case, together with your opinion of the light in which he ought to be considered, and the punishment that ought to be inflicted.

The Judge-Advocate will attend to assist in the examination, who has sundry other papers relative to this matter, which he will lay before the Board.

The "other papers" mentioned by Washington, explained Laurence, he would shortly present to the Board. First it was necessary to read out for the record a fairly lengthy letter written by the prisoner himself, which bore directly on the question at issue. Unsolicited, it had been addressed by Mr. Andre to General Washington the day after his capture, but before his true identity was established.

Turning to Andre, Laurence asked if the prisoner acknowledged writing the letter and having it sent by courier. Readily Andre answered with a smiling yes, of course. He'd written it the evening of the 25th, he said, while being held at South Salem.

LAURENCE: Why in those peculiar circumstances did you think that such a letter, or any letter, to the Commander-in-Chief was necessary?

ANDRE: Sir, I believe the letter will fully answer that question. My captors and guards had repeatedly referred to me as having been a spy. As would any gentleman, I abhorred the imputation of treacherous dealing.

LAURENCE (turning to face the Board): The letter is of some length. But it is certainly the most important document in the case, amounting to what seems a confession. I feel that it should be read into the record without omission.

Greene nodded his concurrence and for the next five minutes only the voice of Laurence was heard in the room:

Sir,

What I have as yet said concerning myself was in the justifiable attempt to be extricated; I am too little accustomed to duplicity to have succeeded.

I beg your Excellency will be persuaded that no alteration in the temper of my mind, or apprehension for my safety, induces me to take the step of addressing you, but that it is to secure myself from an imputation of having assumed a mean character for treacherous purposes or self-interest—a conduct incompatible with the principles that actuated me, as well as with my condition in life.

It is to vindicate my fame that I speak, and not to solicit security.

The person in your possession is Major John Andre, Adjutant-General to the British army.

Lowering the paper, Laurence glanced along the line of generals, all listening attentively. I remind the gentlemen, he said, that at his capture the prisoner went under the name of John Anderson, claiming to be a merchant from New York City. He maintained the disguise for some thirty-five hours, until the writing of this letter, as he says, in custody at South Salem on the evening of the 25th September. He went on reading:

The influence of one commander in the army of his adversary is an advantage taken in war. A correspondence for this purpose I held, as confidential (in the present instance) with his Excellency Sir Henry Clinton. To favor it, I agreed to meet upon ground not within the posts of either army, a person who was to give me intelligence. I came up in the Vulture man of war for this effect, and was fetched, by a boat from the shore, to the beach. Being there, I was told that the approach of day would prevent my return, and that I must be concealed until the next night.

I was in my regimentals, and had fairly risked my person.

Against my stipulation, my intention and without my knowledge beforehand, I was conducted within one of your posts. Your Excellency may conceive my sensation on this occasion, and will imagine how much more I must have been affected, by a refusal to re-conduct me back the next night as I had been brought. Thus become a prisoner I had to concert my escape.

Laurence paused again: As to the fact of Mr. Andre coming ashore in his regimental uniform and thereby risking his person, he omits a relevant fact. Indeed he was wearing his uniform but it was concealed under a plain civilian overcoat, and he soon changed entirely to civilian clothes. He resumed:

I quitted my uniform, was passed another way in the night without the American posts to neutral ground, and informed that I was beyond all armed parties, and left to press for New York. I was taken at Tarrytown by some volunteers.

Thus, as I have had the honor to relate, was I betrayed (being Adjutant-General of the British army) into the vile condition of an enemy in disguise within your posts.

Having avowed myself a British officer, I have nothing to reveal but what relates to myself, which is true on the honor of an officer and a gentleman. The request I have to make your Excellency, and I am conscious I address myself well, is that in any rigor policy may dictate, a decency of conduct towards me may mark that, though unfortunate, I am branded with nothing dishonorable, as no motive could be mine but the service of my King, and as I was involuntarily an imposter.

Another request is that I may be permitted to write an open letter to Sir Henry Clinton, and another to a friend for clothes and linen.

Another pause by Laurence: I should explain, he said, that both letters were permitted, and the clothes sent up from British head-quarters in New York City were given to the prisoner. I may add, as most of you know, that the prisoner has lacked for nothing while in our hands, but has been treated almost as a guest. Unfortunately he chose to end his letter on a rather sour and disappointing note:

I take the liberty to mention the condition of some gentlemen at Charleston, who being either on parole or under protection, were engaged in a conspiracy against us. Tho' their situation is not similar, they are objects who may be set in exchange for me, or are persons whom the treatment I receive might affect.

It is no less, Sir, in a confidence in the generosity of your mind, than on account of your superior station, that I have chosen to importune you with this letter.

During the reading of the letter the faces of the judges gave little sign of emotion or of what they might be thinking. Now nearly all mirrored real annoyance, including that of General Greene who asked that Laurence go back and read again the paragraph near the letter's end about the American prisoners at Charleston. Laurence ran his finger down the paper, then read: "Tho' their situation is not similar, they are objects who may be set in exchange for me, or are persons whom the treatment I receive might affect."

GREENE (staring grim-faced at the prisoner): That sounds very much like a threat of retaliation on innocent soldiers in your hands, depending on our verdict here. You say you wish to be recognized as

General Nathaniel Greene, Washington's own favorite general, who headed the board of fourteen generals that tried Andre.

an officer and a gentleman and you deny having acted in "a mean character." What do you call retaliation on innocent prisoners—I suppose by that you threaten execution—but acting in a *very* mean spirit? Is that the part of a gentleman, of an officer who understands the true point of honor?

Andre, in obvious discomfort, sat silent, his look seeming to say that he sincerely regretted giving in to the impulse to make such a clumsy, useless threat.

GREENE: You say you are "little accustomed to duplicity." How does *that* claim fit with barefaced threats of retaliation, nothing but *revenge*, plain and simple?

Still only silence from the prisoner.

GREENE: You refer to your "condition in life," meaning you enjoy the privileges of a gentleman, well above the common herd, let's say. How does the code of a gentleman fit with—

LAURENCE (interrupting): Your Excellency, may I suggest that questioning of the prisoner be delayed until after my presentation of the evidence, and until Mr. Andre has had a chance for a full reply? He has brought with him a written statement.

As the prosecutor knew, more than most others General Greene had been shocked and disgusted by the treason of his fellow general. He viewed what he called "the hellish plot" to betray West Point as a truly frightening event which if successful would "have given the American cause a deadly wound, if not a fatal stab." In a broadside he published in his General Orders to the army three days before, he had said as much, and also gave his downright opinion that Andre had beyond doubt acted as a spy. In interrupting, Laurence hoped to forestall what seemed a gathering storm.

Greene sat back. Proceed, he instructed Laurence.

GENERAL STARK: One moment . . . Major Andre, in your letter you avoid naming your American conspirator. You say only that you met with "a person who was to give me intelligence." As all the world knows by now that person was our turncoat General Benedict Arnold, who unfortunately made his escape soon after you were apprehended. What was your reason for concealing his name in your letter to General Washington, while admitting everything else?

ANDRE: The letter was written the day following my capture, while I was being held in an American militia outpost. At that moment I had no idea as to whether Arnold had been exposed or was even suspected, didn't know if he was in custody or still at large. I was buying time for him to extricate himself. Also it seemed to me that there was still a chance for our original design of taking possession of West Point to succeed. A slim chance yet worth preserving.

STARK: Yes, that makes sense . . . but in that case, Major, why did you so readily confess your own true identity? Your disguise as Mr. Anderson could not possibly have been penetrated for many days. Admitting who you were did not aid your design.

ANDRE: Sir, as I explain in my letter, I wished to protect my honor as an officer and a gentleman. I wasn't in disguise by choice, I was *betrayed* into that vile condition and—

STARK: But from a British viewpoint shouldn't you have concealed matters as long as possible? Why admit everything as you did, while the situation was still fluid? . . . never mind . . . That's all, Colonel.

Lifting a thin sheaf of paper from the table, Laurence explained that they had been found concealed on Andre's person. Walking over to Andre's table he held the papers out to the prisoner. When you were stopped and searched by three men of our militia, he said, these papers were found. Do you acknowledge them?

ANDRE (throwing a glance at the papers): Yes, sir, I do. I had them in my boots. Inside my stockings under my bare feet. I thought no one would think to look there even if they removed my boots. (Again that casual, confiding tone, betraying not the least sign of doubt or worry.)

LAURENCE (turning back to face the Board): Six documents are involved here. Three are in the handwriting of General Benedict Arnold, who as you know commanded at West Point.

As Laurence described each of the three he held it up for display, then laid it on the table:

The first paper lists the number of troops available at and near West Point, breaking the total down by specific location and numbers of men at each. The second paper gives in detail the condition and

General Benedict Arnold, the arch-traitor, who offered to betray the American stronghold under his command at West Point.

aspect of the West Point fortifications, covering the ten principal posts. The third paper is a copy of the minutes of a War Council held under General Washington three weeks ago at West Point. As you see, it is a lengthy document, and sets out specific American plans for the conduct of the war, at the moment and in the immediate future.

Those three documents, continued Laurence, are written in General Arnold's own handwriting. The three remaining papers are in the form of reports made to General Arnold by two of his officers, Major Bauman, chief of artillery, and Major Villefranche, chief engineer. He held up two of the papers as he went on. Major Bauman supplies a detailed explanation of how and where he would dispose his men in case of an attack, and also a chart showing the number and kind of guns at each of seventeen locations. The report of Major Villefranche gives an estimate of the number of troops, aside from the artillery, needed to defend each fort or reboubt.

Together, the information contained in these papers, finished Laurence, as you gentlemen need not be told, gives an attacking enemy a great advantage, especially where the Commander is himself a traitor who has done his best to weaken the forts and is waiting to surrender, and who—

GREENE (impatiently, his tone demanding): Mr. Andre, how did you come by those six papers? Were they given to you? Did you steal them?

ANDRE (indignantly): Sir, they were given to me.

GREENE: Who gave them to you?

ANDRE: General Arnold. At the same time he warned me to hide them. In my boots, he said.

GREENE: When was this? Where? Please be precise.

ANDRE: (holding up the paper): Sir, those questions and others are answered in the statement I've written, which I should like to read to the court, if I may. Colonel Laurence suggested to me that I might do so.

GREENE (looking at Laurence): Anything else to present?

LAURENCE (holding up a small rectangle of paper): One thing more, Sir. This is a military pass. It was shown by the prisoner to his captors, hoping to be let go. (Looking at Andre) Do you acknowledge owning and showing this pass, which gave you a false identity?

ANDRE: Yes, it is the one I used.

LAURENCE: I shall read it out as self-explanatory. *"Permit Mr. John Anderson to pass the guards to the White Plains or below it as he chuses. He being on public business by my direction. B. Arnold, Major General."*

Laurence turned and handed the pass to General Greene, who glanced at it then passed it along.

I think, said Laurence, we are ready now to hear the prisoner's statement. Greene nodded and Andre picked up the paper. He was allowed to read without interruption:

On the 20th of September I left New York to get on board the *Vulture* in order (as I thought) to meet General Arnold there in the night. No boat, however, came off, and I waited on board until the night of the 21st.

During the day a flag of truce was sent from the *Vulture* to complain of the violation of a military rule in the instance of a boat having been decoyed on shore by a flag, and fired upon. The letter was addressed to General Arnold by Captain Sutherland, but written in my hand and countersigned "J. Anderson, Secretary." Its intent was to indicate my presence on board the *Vulture*.

In the night of the 21st a boat with Mr.———— and two hands came on board in order to fetch Mr. Anderson on shore, and if too late to bring me back, to lodge me until the next night in a place of safety. I went into the boat, landed, and spoke with Arnold. I got on horseback with him to proceed to———— house, and on the way passed a guard I did not expect to see, having Sir Henry Clinton's directions not to go within an enemy's post, or to quit my own dress.

In the morning A. quitted me, having himself made me put the papers I bore between my stockings and feet. Whilst he did it, he expressed a wish that in case of any accident befalling me, that they should be destroyed, which I said of course would be the case, as when I went into the boat I should have them tied about with a string and a stone. Before we parted some mention had been made of my crossing the river, and going by another route; but I objected much against it, and thought it was settled that in the way I came I was also to return.

Mr.———— to my great mortification persisted in his determination of carrying me by the other route; and at the decline of the sun I set out on horseback, passed King's Ferry, and came to Crompond where a party of militia stopped us and advised we should remain. In the morning I came with Mr.———— as far as within two miles and a half of Pine's Bridge, where he said he must part with me, as the Cow-boys infested the road thenceforward.*

I was now near thirty miles from Kingsbridge, and left to the chance of passing that space undiscovered. I got to the neighborhood of Tarrytown, which was far beyond the points described as dangerous, when I was taken by three volunteers who, not satisfied with my pass, rifled me and finding papers made me a prisoner.

I have omitted mentioning that, when I found myself within an enemy's post, I changed my dress.

Putting down the paper, Andre sat back. I thank the gentlemen for permitting me to read my explanation, he said. I'm afraid it is not so complete or so well-expressed as I could have wished, but it was done in rather a hurry last night. I am ready to answer, honestly and openly, any questions you may have.

GREENE: Thank you, Major. I do have some questions, as I'm sure will other members of the Board. As to coming ashore, where exactly did you land for your meeting with Arnold?

ANDRE: It was a rocky beach just below Haverstraw town. Say two miles below Haverstraw. A wooded section rising up from the river. *Outside* the American lines.

GREENE: You say you were brought within our lines by General Arnold. You say it was done against your wishes and without your prior knowledge. Please explain that statement more fully. Are you saying that you were *forced*?

Cowboys was a label given to irregular bands of British sympathizers in Westchester's Neutral Ground. Their opposite numbers were known as *Skinners*.

ANDRE: Sir, I told General Arnold on meeting him that I wished to remain on neutral ground while we talked. Only later when Arnold answered a guard's challenge at the edge of Haverstraw as we went along did I become aware of passing within your lines.

GREENE: But at that point, hearing the guard's challenge, you were aware? You knew it was an American sentry?

ANDRE: Yes, of course. But I—

GREENE (interrupting): Why did you continue? According to your statement your own commander, Sir Henry Clinton, had forbidden you to enter within our lines. Why didn't you stop?

ANDRE: Sir, by then I had no choice. I was committed and—

GREENE (in disbelief): No choice? You were on a horse, supplied by Arnold. You could have turned and ridden the other way.

ANDRE: On that side of the river I knew nothing about the lay of the land, or the disposition of forces of either army. I'd been promised a return directly to the *Vulture*, then was told it was too late to risk it. Dressed as I was in my uniform I could take no chances. If I was to be put back aboard ship the next night, then I needed a secure place to spend the daylight hours.

GENERAL KNOX: So in order to be safe from discovery, you yourself deliberately chose to enter our lines. *You* made the decision.

ANDRE: No, sir, not in the absolute way you imply.

KNOX: You spoke with Arnold there on the shore, then were taken by him inside our lines to the home of Joshua Smith. How long did the meeting on the shore last?

ANDRE: Sir, I said I was taken to a house. I did not say whose house it was.

KNOX: Correct, you didn't say. But we know it was Smith's house, the same man whose name you leave blank in your statement. You know of course that we have Mr. Smith in custody and that he will stand trial in a few days.

From Andre came no reply or comment.

KNOX: How long did your meeting with Arnold last?

ANDRE: I wasn't aware of the time passing. But I know that when I went ashore it was well after midnight, probably after one. We had much to discuss, General Arnold and I—as you can imagine!

There was silence in the room as the judges stared at the prisoner, evidently picturing that shadowy encounter and imagining the hours-long, low-voiced exchanges between the two men.

GENERAL HUNTINGTON: Major, let me ask about your capture. When you were stopped by our militiamen, you say you showed your pass, bearing Arnold's signature, expecting to have no trouble. In your written statement read to us here you say the captors were "not satisfied" with the pass. You say they found those papers by accident as they "rifled" your clothes. Why were they not satisfied with the pass? It seems in order.

ANDRE: I can't say, sir. One of them, their leader, read it, but he just ignored it. He didn't say anything in explanation, just put it in his pocket.

HUNTINGTON: Didn't you protest such treatment, insist on your rights to free passage? It all sounds strangely subdued to me, considering what was at stake for you.

ANDRE: Of course I protested. To no avail. I did think of making a break for freedom but found no chance . . .

HUNTINGTON (turning to Laurence): Colonel, do we know why those men rejected the pass? I understand the three have finally been located and are being questioned. Have they been asked about the pass yet?

LAURENCE: Sir, it's not a question of rejecting the pass. The men claim that the prisoner when stopped said something about his being British, or about favoring the British cause. The pass he produced only after that, which made them suspicious. Their leader—his name is John Paulding—admits that if Major Andre had shown the pass in the first instance they'd have had no choice but to let him go. But he didn't.

HUNTINGTON: What about it, major? Did you first say something about being British? I can't imagine you doing that, not in such critical circumstances.

ANDRE (after a pause): Those first moments after I was stopped are rather hazy, and I've had little rest since then. It's entirely possible that I said something like that in passing. Your militiamen weren't in uniform, you know. On first sight I couldn't be sure *who* they were, so close to our lines in New York City. But my memory is confused . . .

HUNTINGTON: After ignoring the pass they searched you, or as you prefer, they "rifled" you, at last finding the papers. At that point, I understand, you offered them a bribe, which they also ignored.

ANDRE: True, the usual thing . . . I don't wish to denigrate my captors, who are sturdy yeomen all, but I can't help feeling that if I'd had a few hundred pounds in my pocket at the time I might have gone free—

GREENE (emphatically): The captors claim otherwise, Major! In the circumstances I think we'll take *their* word.

HUNTINGTON: You offered them a substantial bribe and said you'd arrange to get the money to them. They refused. Does that cover it?

ANDRE: So much is true, yes.

GENERAL GLOVER (looking up from his copious notes): Mr. Andre, I see that in your original letter to General Washington you say that when you came ashore, and I quote, "I was in my regimentals, and had fairly risked my person." Mr. Laurence tells us that you also had on an overcoat. What sort?

ANDRE: It was what they call a surtout.

GLOVER: That's an extra-long, high-collared greatcoat, a civilian garment, not a military one. Where did you get it? Was it your own?

ANDRE: I borrowed it at the last minute from one of the men on the *Vulture*. I had not thought to bring one.

GLOVER: By wearing it you considerably reduced the risk you say you took in coming ashore in uniform, didn't you?

ANDRE: Slightly, I suppose. It was my friends on the ship who insisted. Also I was told that I should conceal my identity from the American boatmen, the rowers.

GLOVER: You mean you were ready to come ashore *without* the overcoat, while wearing your uniform? That hardly sounds like a prudent move.

ANDRE: The original idea was for a private meeting to take place on the shore at night. From there I was to go directly back to the ship, still under cover of darkness. So you—

LAFAYETTE (interrupting): *Why* didn't you go directly back?

ANDRE: Our talk wasn't finished, and General Arnold suggested that we continue at a safe house he had ready in Haverstraw. There was also some difficulty about the lateness of the hour and the adverse tides. I could go the next night just as easily, Arnold said. You realize that by then I was effectively in Arnold's hands. In a way I had become a prisoner behind American lines, as I say in my letter to General Washington.

LAFAYETTE: A prisoner? How so? Why would—

ANDRE: It amounted to that, Sir.

LAFAYETTE: But you were in a conspiracy with the American commander! How could you be a prisoner of your confederate?

ANDRE: Sir, I use the word in a loose sense. I was a prisoner of circumstances not of my own making.

GLOVER: At any time after you went ashore from the *Vulture*, up to the time you reached the safe house in Haverstraw, did you remove the overcoat?

ANDRE: No, sir, I kept it on, buttoned up.

GLOVER: So you were wearing it when you and Arnold on entering Haverstraw passed the American sentry?

ANDRE: Of course! Passing the guard-post with my uniform uncovered would have been silly, even accompanied by Arnold (again that easy, confiding smile).

GLOVER (his tone doubtful): Where then was the risk you claim?

GREENE (looking along the line of generals): Thank you, General. Anyone else?

GENERAL PARSONS: About your clothes, Major. As I understand it you changed to civilian dress while in the safe house at Haverstraw, Joshua Smith's house—strike that, I know you did not specify whose house. But while in the house at Haverstraw, within American lines, you made the change. This involved removing your red uniform tunic, your shirt, neckcloth, and vest, donning replacements. Your buff trousers and military boots you retained.

ANDRE: That describes it, sir.

PARSONS: Those distinctive, white-topped military boots—I see you are still wearing them—shouldn't they have been replaced?

ANDRE: I could find no others to fit me.

PARSONS: Especially since they had to contain not only your feet, but six folded documents as well. Who provided the civilian clothes? Since the change wasn't part of the original plan, I assume it wasn't Arnold.

ANDRE: If you don't mind, I prefer not to answer that.

PARSONS: Of course it was Joshua Hett Smith, wasn't it?

From Andre came no reply as he sat upright at the table, looking pleasantly at his questioner.

PARSONS: Where did you leave your discarded regimentals?

Still only silence.

PARSONS: Let me make sure that I have this right. In your letter to General Washington you explain that you donned civilian dress in order, as you say, "to concert my escape." On horseback, with Smith as your guide, you traversed Haverstraw, crossed the river at King's Ferry, then proceeded south through the Neutral Ground,

Andre's own sketch of the scene as he arrived for his secret nighttime meeting with Benedict Arnold on the river's western shore.

where you were taken when not far from your own lines. You admit that you were inside American lines in disguise, that you passed two American guard-posts in disguise, on either side of the river. Not only were you posing as an American civilian all this while, but you also carried a pass made out by General Arnold to you in an assumed name, that of Anderson. You were both disguised and using a false identity.

ANDRE (his tone mild): Those are the facts, sir. But I assert and must insist that you are putting the worst face on them. You need to consider the situation, the reasons that led to my change of dress . . . May I also point out that there is a factual error contained in General Washington's order to the Board read out at the start this morning?

A recent view of Andre's landing place on the Hudson shore looking east. The low-lying Teller's Point can be seen, and beyond it the Westchester hills.

I was certainly *not* captured within your lines. I was taken a mile or so short of Tarrytown, which is neutral territory between the lines, under the control of neither army. In that case it cannot be said that I was in disguise when taken. In neutral territory a man may wear whatever clothing he chooses, military or civilian.

GREENE (throwing an annoyed look at Laurence): Colonel?

LAURENCE (contritely): The capture *was* made on Neutral Ground, sir. We regret the error. How it affects the question of disguise I leave to the Board. In my view it's of no consequence.

GREENE (apologetically): Major, we do sincerely regret the mistake. But it is not material to the charge . . . Just to be clear—wherever it happened, when stopped you were in civilian clothes?

ANDRE: I was. The same I put on in Haverstraw.

GREENE (looking around): Any questions?

GENERAL HAND (his tone friendly, with a trace of brogue): Sir, there's something I'm not clear on. *Why* didn't you return to the ship directly from shore that *second* night? Why go back by land, taking so much time and running such a risk?

ANDRE: I was told that the *Vulture* had dropped downriver after being fired on from the opposite shore. It was down too far to reach in safety by rowboat.

HAND: Yes, it's true, the ship was indeed fired on from a small battery ashore. The officer at Teller's Point got sick of looking at that British ensign tantalizing him from the ship's forepeak, as I've heard. But Major, was the ship really too far down to reach?

ANDRE: I was told so. Please remember, sir, I had not the control of these matters, the means and ways of coming and going in those circumstances.

HAND: If you'd gotten back aboard that ship in the river, instead of going that roundabout way on land, the game would've been up with us. You had troops ready to move, I'm sure.

ANDRE (after a pause): So we hoped and expected, sir. We had three regiments ready aboard vessels in New York City. They were to attack upriver the moment the wind was fair.

HAND: Why exactly did you meet with Arnold? To get hold of those documents? Was there something else?

ANDRE: We'd been in touch with Arnold by secret correspondence for some time, well over a year. We had to be sure that our contact really *was* Benedict Arnold. The whole thing might have been an American plot to entrap us, to draw our troops into an ambush. Someone had to meet face-to-face with Arnold. Not every day, you'll agree, does a major-general offer to defect, delivering his post as well.

HAND (shaking his head): I can't help thinking how strange it is,

Major, that with so much depending on it, you allowed yourself to be shunted off on that long return journey by land instead of striking straight from shore to ship, even if you had to swim! Thank God you didn't! But why—

GREENE (interrupting): General Hand, that raises what I think a crucial question, the possibility that a flag of truce was used. (Turning to Andre) Major, in your letter to General Washington you don't claim the protection of a flag, nor in your statement to this court. I have here a letter written three days ago by your commander, Sir Henry Clinton, to General Washington. It asserts that you came ashore under a flag of truce and therefore must be released immediately. Clinton says he has his information directly from General Arnold, who as you know made his escape on hearing of your capture and is now in the city. Sir Henry sends a copy of Arnold's statement, which includes this language:

> Major Andre . . . is assuredly under the protection of a flag of truce sent by me to him for the purpose of a conversation, which I requested to hold with him relating to myself, and which I wished to communicate through that officer to your Excellency [Sir Henry]. I commanded at the time at West Point and had an undoubted right to send my flag of truce for Major Andre who came to me under that protection . . .

Let's take this slowly, Major. Think back to the night you came ashore, eight days ago. In or on the rowboat that came to the *Vulture*, and then carried you to the western shore, was there a white flag flying? A flag of truce? I caution you to think well before you reply. Take as much time as you like to consider your answer.

ANDRE (barely hesitating): About General Arnold's statement I make no comment or observation. But I saw no such flag. I cannot claim that I came ashore under that sanction. I say that I saw no such flag flying, neither as I stepped down into the rowboat from the ship, nor as the rowers pulled for the beach.

GREENE: That's your final statement?

ANDRE: It is. I'll add what I think should be obvious, and which is wholly germane. If I'd come to land under a flag of truce, then certainly I might have gone safely back aboard under it that same night, or at any time.

GREENE (with an approving shake of his head): In truth, Major, I'm very glad to hear you say that. In *those* circumstances a flag of truce wouldn't save you. It would make matters very much worse. It would leave a brand of infamy on your name. (Greene gazed sharply at the prisoner, waiting for a reaction. None came.) As you know very well, Major, flags of truce are not meant to cover treason. They don't protect conspirators. No honorable man, no gentleman, would ever think to prostitute this needed custom of war, which depends entirely on a moment of trust between adversaries. Of course the traitor Arnold was lying. Sir Henry must have guessed it too, but was grasping at straws. Understandable . . . and yet Sir Henry doesn't hesitate to lay this heavy burden on *your* name and fame. It is obvious, Major, that Sir Henry expects you to *agree* that a flag was flying . . .

Again Greene paused, waiting. But Andre sat in silence, looking uncertain and uncomfortable while staring steadily at Greene, giving no sign of making a reply or offering comment. For a long thirty seconds no sound or movement disturbed the room.

GENERAL HOWE: Maybe there's another way of looking at all this, Major. Maybe Sir Henry sees you as only a messenger, a courier sent to pick up and return certain documents and information. Were you *that*, Major, a mere messenger, having no real or substantial knowledge of the plot or its inner workings? If you were only an innocent courier, perhaps expected also to verify Arnold's identity, and if a flag of truce was flying . . .

ANDRE (blurting his answer): No, sir! I was *not* a mere messenger or courier! From the start I handled all the correspondence with General Arnold. All subsequent negotiations passed through me with Sir Henry's approval. That includes discussion as to how much Arnold was to be paid. Also when and how West Point should be attacked. I can't claim innocence in that regard.

HOWE: You were at the center of the plot?

ANDRE (almost proudly): I was.

HOWE: And no flag of truce was flying?

ANDRE: There was no flag, sir, no flag at all.

GREENE: Major, would you like to add anything further, I mean on any aspect of this matter? Please take your time to consider. We wish to leave no point unexamined.

His eyes dropping to the table, for a moment Andre paused, thinking. Then his gaze came up, and with a broad smile, his tone confident, he replied, No, sir, there isn't. What I have already said and written about myself I leave to operate with the Board. May I also thank the Board for its gracious consideration of me and of my rather strange situation, the accidental and unintended nature of which I trust I have made clear. My actions since finding myself in Haverstraw, an eventuality never contemplated, have really been quite inadvertent . . . but I have said enough, and I shall try your patience no longer.

As he spoke, his dark eyes, swept slowly along the line of soberly attentive faces, frankly searching for a glimmer of sympathy. None gave even a hint of agreeing or disagreeing with what he said.

GREENE (addressing the Board): Gentlemen, we now have enough to start deliberations. We have the prisoner's own testimony on record, and the various documents submitted in evidence. So far, no essential item of the main charge has been disputed, so as of now there's no need to call witnesses. (Turning to Andre) Thank you, Major. We appreciate your cooperation and your admirable candour.

You will now be returned to your room. Should we find that we need you again, you'll be warned in good time, informed of our concern, and allowed to prepare. Thank you.

Lifting a hand, Greene signaled to the guards standing at the rear of the chamber.

IT WAS WELL on in the afternoon when the fourteen generals, after a quick lunch, straggled by twos and threes back to the Old Dutch Church. The line of tables had been rearranged into a semi-circle, General Greene's chair at its center.

Gentlemen, said Greene as the others took their seats, the Commander expects a decision from us no later than this evening, and I think we may accommodate him. Let me repeat his instructions as read to us this morning: "After a careful examination you will be pleased *as speedily as possible* to report a precise state of his case, together with your opinion of the light in which he ought to be considered, and the punishment that ought to be inflicted."

Now, recalling this morning's testimony, added Greene, it's clear that two main points are to be judged. *First,* was Major Andre, a British officer, at any time within our lines secretly and in a deliberate disguise? If so, how did he get there and is he culpable as to the condition? *Second,* do the papers he carried, containing secret intelligence of our military status and plans, prove his deliberate role in Arnold's treason? Together do these charges, if sustained, mark him as having acted the part of a spy, under the technical and specific definition of that label?

Who will begin? finished Greene, looking around.

During the next four or five hours, perhaps as many as seven or eight, every aspect of the Arnold-Andre conspiracy was analyzed in a free-wheeling discussion. Regrettably, no record of the lengthy session survives, if any was kept, nor did any of the participants leave written comments afterward, so no reconstruction of what was said, and by whom, in those critical hours can be attempted. Yet the main points, as laid out and guided by General Greene, are fairly obvious. They can be summed up under five headings:

1. The meeting with Arnold, exactly when and where it took place; reasons for the particular time and locale chosen; its purpose and result;
2. Andre's part in the meeting with Arnold, how it should be viewed in light of approved international law and custom, that is, whether undoubtedly clandestine and criminal, or mitigated by any other factors;
3. The question of his altering his appearance, when and how and where done, and under what compulsion; effect of the disguise on his status at different moments during his self-styled "escape";
4. His overt use of a feigned identity; his having an official military pass which argued both deep involvement and careful preparation; the fact that the spurious pass if shown to the captors at once would have allowed the prisoner's escape;
5. His illegal possession of certain documents supplying important military information to the enemy, documents not carried openly but hidden away on the prisoner's person.

In discussion among the earnest Board members these matters would have been refined down to their minutest slivers of meaning, connotation and annotation. Despite later English claims, none of the judges was out for revenge. In fact, most of them, the younger ones in particular, seem to have searched for ways to avoid the most serious conclusions on the evidence. Whether in the lengthy discussions that afternoon there occurred any real disagreement on the part of one or two members, as rumor later claimed, whether the final vote was indeed unanimous, as it appears, are things now beyond knowing. The only certainty is the written verdict itself—signed by all fourteen judges plus the Judge-Advocate—as it was delivered to Washington at the De Windt house late that evening:

> THE BOARD HAVING considered the letter from his Excellency General Washington respecting Major Andre, Adjutant-General to the British Army, the confession of Major Andre, and the papers produced to them, REPORT to his Excellency the Commander-in-Chief the following facts, which appear to them relative to Major Andre.
>
> First, that he came on shore from the Vulture sloop of war in the night of the twenty-first of September instant, on an interview with General Arnold, in a private and secret manner.
>
> Secondly, that he changed his dress within our lines, and under a feigned name, and in a disguised habit, passed our works at Stony and Verplank's Points, the evening of the twenty-second of September instant, and was taken the morning of the twenty-third of September instant, at Tarrytown in a disguised habit, being then on his way to New York; and when taken he had in his possession several papers which contained intelligence for the enemy.
>
> The Board having maturely considered these facts, DO ALSO REPORT to his Excellency General Washington, that Major Andre, Adjutant-General to the British army, ought to be considered as a spy from the enemy, and that agreeably to the law and usage of nations, it is their opinion, he ought to suffer death.

In his room at the Mabie Tavern Andre had been waiting since about two that afternoon to hear whether he was to live or die. He understood that the decision of the Court was not binding but would be submitted for approval to the Commander-in-Chief. Whether, when the court concluded its deliberations, he was told about it, if he knew at what hour the crucial document reached Washington, is not on record.

All that is known with certainty is that by midnight the prisoner still had heard nothing, and that sometime in the small hours he fell into a troubled sleep.

III

ANDRE FOR ARNOLD?

I n Washington's restless, overburdened mind there burned a single
thought, and it had nothing to do with Andre or his fate. It was
about Benedict Arnold and his now-fierce hatred of the man. Greatly
admiring his subordinate's fighting qualities, displayed repeatedly on
the battlefield and especially against Burgoyne at Saratoga in 1777,
he had done everything he could to promote and elevate him in rank
and influence. It was at Arnold's specific request that he'd given him
command of West Point. Now what he wanted above all else was to
get his hands on the arch-traitor and make him pay for his despicable
act of treason in an official public hanging.

Arnold at the moment, however, having made a hairbreadth, last-
minute escape downriver from West Point to the *Vulture*, was safe
among the British in New York City, apparently inaccessible by ordinary means. Sending in an undercover team to assassinate the traitor, as some urged, would probably work. But that was the last thing
Washington wanted, and he gave strict orders prohibiting any such
attempt. Arnold he wanted alive, wanted his official execution to
serve as an example for other possible deserters, hoped that the sight
of Arnold dangling at the end of a rope would restore some of the
ragged American army's badly damaged prestige.

Two possibilities presented themselves, each in turn receiving the Commander's attention. First, he could send in a team to kidnap Arnold. Entering New York City by stealth, waylaying Arnold by night at home or in the street, and transporting him across the river to the American camp north of Paulus Hook (now Jersey City) shouldn't be too difficult for a couple of intrepid men.

Second, he could use Andre in some sort of exchange. Of course, as Washington was well aware, a straightforward exchange, a simple swap of the two men, was out of the question. The British, even if so inclined, could never openly return a defector against his will, especially one of Arnold's rank and fame. But they very well might, in order to save their admired young hero, be willing to engage in a less public, less visible arrangement of some sort. Arnold now held little real attraction for the British. West Point had been the plot's real target. Without West Point, Arnold's value for the British had rapidly dwindled, the sensation and significance of his defection hardly worth the half-million dollars he'd been paid.

Certainly in those circumstances a veiled exchange was worth trying for. If nothing came of it there was always the kidnapping.

Early on the morning of Saturday, September 30, Washington with his own hand wrote a letter to the British Commander in New York, General Sir Henry Clinton. It was a belated reply to Clinton's letter to Washington of the 26th, in which he claimed a flag of truce for Andre. Brief and carefully worded, it tells only enough to show how dire was Andre's predicament:

> . . . Major Andre was taken under such circumstances as would have justified the most summary proceedings against him. I determined however to refer his case to the examination of a Board of General Officers, who have reported on his free and voluntary confession and letters, "That he came on shore from the Vulture sloop of war, in the night of the twenty-first of September instant" etc. etc. . . .

From these proceedings it is evident Major Andre was employed in the execution of measures very foreign to the objects of flags of truce, and such as they were never meant to authorize or countenance in the most distant degree; and this gentleman confessed with the greatest candor, in the course of his examination, "That it was impossible for him to suppose he came ashore under the sanction of a flag."

In reality the letter wasn't important. It was merely an excuse, allowing Washington to send another, quite different message, this one to be delivered quietly in person by the courier. Give me Arnold, it said in effect, and I'll give you Andre.

Along with his own letter to Clinton, with fairly subtle calculation Washington sent a second letter, written by Andre and addressed to his superior in New York City. Composed the evening before as Andre waited to hear his fate, it was an unusual missive, not only in itself but as to its real or underlying purpose, as well as for Washington's reason for allowing it. Well-known ever since its publication some years later, it is often extolled as a model of sensitive expression, and as showing Andre's gentlemanly spirit of solicitous gratitude toward the general who had shown him such favor. It was that, and more: knowing it would be read by his captors before being sent, Andre was actually using it in another bid to influence his judges, expressing in apparently sincere, offhand form the claims he'd already made in court.

"Your Excellency is doubtless already apprized of the manner in which I was taken," he wrote, "and possibly of the serious light in which my conduct is considered." He has been given permission to write in order "to remove from your breast any suspicion that I could imagine I was bound by your Excellency's orders to expose myself" to unnecessary danger:

The events of coming within an enemy's posts, and of changing my dress, which led me to my present situation, were contrary

to my intentions, as they were to your orders; and the circuitous route which I took to return was imposed (perhaps una-
voidably) without alternative upon me . . .

In addressing myself to your Excellency on this occasion,
the force of all my obligations to you, and of the attachment
and gratitude I bear you recurs to me. With all the warmth of
my heart, I give you thanks for your Excellency's profuse kindness to me; and I send you the most earnest wishes for your
welfare which a faithful, affectionate, and respectful attendant
can frame . . .

I receive the greatest attention from his Excellency General
Washington, and from every person under whose charge I happen to be placed.

If there was a chance that Clinton's heart could be melted by
thoughts of his youthful favorite dying cruelly on a scaffold, so that
to save him he'd be readier to surrender Arnold, Washington decided, those elegantly expressed sentiments might give it a shove.

The door of Washington's office opened and an aide came in to
report that Captain Ogden had arrived as ordered. Send him in, said
Washington. Commander of an elite company of dragoons, Captain
Aaron Ogden, twice wounded in combat, was known to Washington
as one of the most capable young officers in the army. Holding out
a small packet, Washington directed that he was to take his whole
company, all twenty-five men, and ride at top speed for the British
position at Paulus Hook, where he was to deliver the packet to the
post commander. He was to request the commander to send it immediately across the river to General Clinton in New York City,
explaining that he would wait for a reply.

Picking up a small scrap of paper from his desk, Washington
handed it to Ogden. Written on it was a short message, containing
only twenty-two words. Memorize this, said Washington, then de-
stroy the scrap. At Paulus Hook you will tell this message exactly as
memorized to the British commander and ask him to relay it in the

same way to General Clinton, bringing back whatever reply Clinton will send. Ogden was then to ride, again at top speed, for Tappan, coming on ahead of his company when in safe territory. The distance to be covered each way was about forty miles. If there were no incidents—British patrols might be roaming anywhere below Hackensack—Ogden should reach the Hook by early afternoon. Allowing a couple of hours for the business with Clinton and for his reply to be received, Ogden should be back in Tappan by nightfall. In any case he was to lose no time either way.

Asking no questions, Ogden accepted the packet and the scrap of paper, and with a salute and a yes, sir! turned and left the office.

For a while after Ogden's departure Washington sat quietly looking out the window at the rolling countryside, the greens just starting to fade to a scatter of browns. Picking up the report of the Board of Inquiry on Andre he read it again, going slowly over every item. From the report and from his own knowledge it was clear to him that much of what happened to the British officer had been unintended, that he'd been led by others. It was also clear that Andre, if he'd wanted to, could have refused to be led. Clearest of all was one crucial fact—unintended or not, accidental or not, Andre's every move was unquestionably that of an out-and-out spy. Reaching for a pen he took a piece of paper and wrote:

> The Commander-in-Chief approves of the opinion of the Board of General Officers respecting Major Andre, and orders that the execution of Major Andre take place tomorrow at five o'clock P.M.

THERE WERE NO INCIDENTS on the way down to Paulus Hook. After some four hours of alternate galloping and resting the horses, Ogden alone under a flag of truce was admitted to the British fort. The post commander, he was told, was not then available. Would he care to join the British officers for lunch while he waited? Two anxious hours later the commander returned and Ogden was taken to his office.

With the door closed and the two of them alone, Ogden handed over the packet, explaining who had sent it. He also had a verbal message, he said, for General Clinton. Would the commander be so good as to carry it to Sir Henry when delivering the packet?

Of course.

Leaning over the commander's desk, Ogden lowered his voice: "If Sir Henry will *in any way* suffer Washington to get General Arnold within his power, Major Andre will be immediately released."

The commander looked up sharply but showed no surprise. Does this come from Washington himself, he asked.

I'm instructed by the highest levels of command to say only that much. You may deliver the message to Sir Henry in confidence.

Abruptly standing up, the officer went to the door and called an aide. Take Captain Ogden to the officers' lounge. To Ogden as he went out he said please wait there while I'm gone.

It was a long wait, apparently from the available evidence some three hours. When the commander did reappear he motioned Ogden with him into his office. Sir Henry had called a council meeting, he explained, and that took time, but he had his answer. In reference to the verbal message he was instructed to reply that nothing like that could be done. Deserters were never given up, no matter who they were. It was Army policy. Then unexpectedly the commander held out an envelope, saying only that it should be delivered to General Washington.

Captain Ogden thanked the officer, saluted, and left.

Darkness had fallen by the time Ogden knocked at the door of the De Windt house, the hour being almost ten o'clock, but inside Washington was anxiously waiting. Obviously disappointed when he heard Clinton's spoken reply, he eagerly broke the wax seal on the letter. What he read brought a grim smile of satisfaction over his strong-featured face. Upon reading Washington's letter, said Clinton,

> . . . I am persuaded the Board of General Officers to whom you referred the case of Major Andre, cannot have been rightly

informed of all the circumstances on which a judgment ought to be formed . . . for this reason I send his Excellency Lieutenant-General Robertson, and two other gentlemen, to give you a true state of facts, and to declare to you my sentiments and resolutions.

   They will set out to-morrow as early as wind and tide will permit, and will wait near Dobb's Ferry for your permission and safe conduct, to meet your Excellency or such persons as you may appoint, to converse with them on this subject . . .

Clinton wanted to parley! The spoken reply he sent was only a blind. There was still a chance.

Washington's first move was to issue a stay of execution for Andre, delaying it one day to Monday, October 2. The hour he moved up from five P.M. to noon. That allowed a good twenty or so hours for meeting Clinton's man and negotiating.

Sending for Greene—whose hatred of Arnold, he knew, matched his own—he had his favorite general read the letter. At first light, he directed, Greene was to set out for Sneden's Landing, on the shore opposite Dobbs Ferry. When he reached there the British schooner might or might not be anchored in mid-stream. If not it would appear presently. He was to allow only one man to come ashore, General Robertson. As a preliminary or a veil, he might discuss the question of Andre's guilt but was not to treat seriously of the question. Whatever Robertson might propose he was to listen to carefully. If it embraced a firm offer to surrender Arnold in return for Andre, Green should immediately give a conditional acceptance, then send a messenger racing back to Tappan for approval. The distance between Sneden's and Tappan was less than four miles, a gallop of little more than ten minutes.

   Accompanied by two of his own aides and also by Washington's aide, Alexander Hamilton, Greene reached Sneden's Landing in good time on the morning of October 1, an open stretch of ground along the shore. No ship was in sight and several hours passed before it appeared, beating upwind from downriver. Anchored at Dobbs Ferry, it sent a boat ashore with a flag of truce to see if the Americans had responded to Clinton's invitation. Greene sent it back with orders to bring Robertson ashore, with an aide if he wished. Soon the two generals were standing face to face.

The exchange at first was stiff and halting. When Robertson questioned the Board's decision as to Andre's guilt, Greene quickly replied that "the case of an *acknowledged* spy admits no official discussion." When Robertson began to insist that Andre had gone ashore under the protection of a flag of truce sent by Arnold, Greene took from his pocket the letter written by Andre to Washington in which he denied being a spy. Greene pointed out that it amounted to a full confession, and mentioned no flag. Robertson countered that the letter had been written while Andre was in a "low-spirited" condition, and had thus misinterpreted the facts. Everything Andre did ashore had been at the direction and under the protection of General Arnold.

This sparked from Greene a more heated reply. It was ridiculous, he growled, to claim that Arnold as commanding officer "had an undoubted right" to send flags of truce and issue official orders while engaged in acts of treason. The instant that Arnold determined in his heart to betray his post and his trust, at that instant he lost all authority. Anything and everything he did as a traitor was invalidated by his intention to betray. Further, Andre himself had admitted there'd been no flag of truce, and that was that. The Americans would take Andre's word for it, rather than Arnold's.

"No military Casuist in Europe," insisted Robertson, pressing the attack, "would call Andre a spy." Wouldn't the fairest thing be to submit the whole question to impartial judges, competent men neither English nor American? The French general Rochambeau, with the American army, and the German General Knyphausen, with the English, were professional soldiers of integrity, familiar with military usage.

No, sir, said Greene with finality.

In British hands, went on Robertson calmly after a moment's pause, were many important American prisoners, civilian and military, including the President of the U.S. Congress, Henry Laurens. If Andre were allowed to come back with him on the ship he could guarantee that one or more of these prisoners, any that Washington cared to name, would be promptly released.

No, sir. (How long will he keep this up, wondered Greene. When will he get to the point?)

A slight tone of annoyance tinged Robertson's voice. General Clinton, he said abruptly, had always shown "a merciful disposition" to any Americans in his power. Wouldn't Washington consider "a return of good officers"?

Greene stood in silence, looking at the ground. The two had been talking for almost an hour. Now Robertson sighed and with a shrug stated that he had no more to discuss, that he'd covered all that he'd been deputized to treat. Wouldn't Greene give some basis for a hope of accommodation?

Isn't there one thing more, asked Greene, adding in plain words, if you want Andre back you know very well how to get him—give us Arnold. Isn't that why you came here?

Shaking his head, Robertson, as he later claimed, answered "with a look only, which threw Greene into confusion" (what Robertson saw in Greene's face at that moment wasn't confusion. It was surprise mixed with sore disappointment. Apparently the traitor was beyond his reach).

Taking a letter from his pocket, Robertson explained that it was written by General Arnold at the request of Sir Henry. It's addressed to General Washington he said, but I'm allowed to show it to you here at my discretion. His manner had become curiously diffident, almost apologetic, as if he felt a little embarrassed. He handed the letter to Greene.

Most of it covered, again, the bothersome topics of flags of truce, safe conduct passes, and the question of Arnold's authority to act as

he did. This Greene hurried over impatiently. Then in growing resentment and anger he found himself reading these words:

> ... if after this just and candid representation of Major Andre's
> case, the Board of General Officers adhere to their opinion, I
> shall suppose it dictated by passion and resentment, and if that
> gentleman should suffer the severity of their sentence I shall
> think myself bound by every tie of Duty and Honor to retaliate
> on such unhappy persons of your army as shall fall within my
> power ...
>
> Suffer not an unjust sentence to touch the life of Major
> Andre. But if this warning be disregarded, and he should suffer,
> I call Heaven and Earth to witness that your Excellency will
> be justly answerable for the Torrent of Blood that may be spilt
> in consequence.

When he finished reading, Greene barely glanced at Robertson as
he held the letter out. But instead of handing it back, he opened his
fingers and let it flutter to the ground at Robertson's booted feet.

Take the general back to the ship, he said to the aide as he turned
and walked away.

"I FLATTER MYSELF that I have never been illiberal," said Andre in
his usual studied way, managing to combine both compliment and
condescension, "but if there were any remains of prejudice in my
mind, my present experience must obliterate them."

He was talking with Hamilton in his room at the Mabie Tavern.
Also present were two of his regular guards, Captain Hughes and
Ensign Tomlinson. The remark—correctly interpreted it means, I'm
astonished to find myself so well treated by these rude, crude colo-
nials—was made on the morning of September 30, before any news
had come of the court's decision and while Andre still felt sure of
escaping conviction as a spy. It was duly recorded and reported and

always thereafter taken as a graceful compliment paid by the gentlemanly prisoner to his admiring captors and judges. It must have been his manner in speaking, that insinuating charm so often noted by visitors, that let him get away with such sallies, which he did fairly often.

With Hamilton that morning Andre fell into a sentimental mood and was soon talking freely of the girl back in England he hoped to marry when his American service was over. Honora Sneyd was her name, a lovely young blue-eyed brunette who lived in Litchfield, where Andre had courted her. They'd been torn apart by his military duties, and his dearest possession was a miniature he'd painted of her before leaving England (if only he could hold it, see it now! But it was in his quarters in New York City). Hamilton, himself just then engaged to a beautiful girl, listened in deep sympathy, agreeing that such a separation must weigh heavily on so sensitive a heart.

Through Hamilton (and others to whom Andre told the story), the legend of the lovely Honora worked its inevitable way into the Andre saga, in the nineteenth century becoming one of its best-known features. But it was mostly a lie. As is now known, there was indeed a young woman named Honora Sneyd who lived in Litchfield. Andre had indeed courted her, did ask for her hand—and was refused. Soon after that Honora quite happily married another of her many suitors, leaving Andre more chagrined than really disappointed. Not for six years, the time he'd been serving in America, had Andre received any news of his old flame. Especially he did not know that, two months before he told the story to Hamilton, Honora had died in childbirth.

By noon of the 30th Andre received another visitor, the prosecutor Colonel Laurence, and with that his manner changed abruptly. The Board of Generals, said Laurence, had unanimously found him to be a spy. Washington had set the evening of the next day at five o'clock for the sentence to be carried out. At the unexpected news

Andre visibly recoiled, then for several minutes, his composure lost, he paced the floor in silence, "his flesh seeming to crawl upon his bones." At last he regained a measure of control and managed to get off another of his typical remarks. "I avow no guilt," he said to Laurence in a shaky voice, "but I'm resigned to my fate."

However, he suffered with the thought of imminent death for no more than ten or so hours. Before midnight of the 30th he'd been informed, again by Colonel Laurence, of Washington's decision to postpone the hanging. When he heard the reason for the delay—a meeting between the Americans and Sir Henry's envoy—he was sure that the worst was over. If nothing else, a prisoner exchange (of course not for Arnold, which he knew was out of the question), would save him. Sir Henry, he was aware, had a good number of Americans in his control, many of whom Washington would like to have returned.

That night, for the first time in a week, he slept fairly well. Next morning, October 1, while the two generals were negotiating at Sneden's Landing, he entertained a succession of visitors, beginning with Major-General the Marquis de LaFayette. Younger than Andre by six years, as one of the judges at the inquiry, as he later admitted, LaFayette had "truly suffered in condemning" the prisoner. But on the evidence he'd had no choice. Now, speaking face-to-face with the man he'd helped sentence to death, he felt even sorrier, and the reason is obvious. For this encounter with a member of the French nobility, Andre exerted himself to make just the right impression, in just the right ways, including being on easy terms with those in high places, and it appears that he succeeded.

"He was a charming man, the confidant and friend of General Clinton," wrote LaFayette afterwards. During the visit "He conducted himself in a manner so frank, so noble, so delicate that . . . I had the foolishness to let myself acquire a strong affection for him." Recalling the affirmative vote he'd cast at the inquiry, he "could not prevent myself from regretting it deeply."

Exactly how in that small, sparcely furnished room at the Mabie Tavern—with what glib words, what practiced facial expressions, what facile body language standing or seated—Andre was able to convey the qualities necessary for impressing the aristocratic La-Fayette—nobility and delicacy—would be interesting to know.

Another visitor that same morning was the already well-disposed Major Tallmadge. Now he found the man he'd been guarding so long to be almost without equal, talking easily and openly of the failed plot, and how he'd expected to win from it no more than "military glory, the applause of his king and country, and perhaps a brigadier-ship." After the hour or so the two spent talking, the visitor left feeling so "attached" to the voluble prisoner "that I can remember no instance where my affections were so fully absorbed in any man."

Back in his own quarters Tallmadge wrote to a friend in high admiration of Andre, who during the visit had been "as cheerful as if he was going to an Assembly." If, in the end, Andre did suffer the extreme penalty, "I am sure he will go to the gallows less fearful for his fate and with less concern than I shall behold the tragedy. Had he been tried by a Court of Ladies, he is so genteel, handsome, polite a young gentleman that I am confident they would have acquitted him."

In the quiet periods between visitors that day, the 1st, Andre passed the time with one of his favorite pursuits, sketching, at which he was adept. With ink and paper, he made two drawings, both re-vealing a true skill at composition and perspective, both pictures centering on himself.

The first was a night scene showing the hilly Hudson shore at Haverstraw, with a rowboat in the foreground carrying two passengers (Andre himself and the man who'd been sent by Arnold to fetch him, Joshua Smith, of course not so identified).

The second showed Andre dressed in his regimental uniform, seated beside a small, round table, the one he had in his room at the tavern. Knees crossed, one arm thrown casually over the chair back,

Major Benjamin Tallmadge, in a contemporary sketch. Put in charge of the prisoner Andre, he soon fell under the Englishman's spell, believing his lies about the captors.

he is eminently relaxed and comfortable, the face serene. As the pen flew over the paper, the guard, Ensign Tomlinson, peered over Andre's shoulder, watching fascinated. When the drawing was finished, with a smile Andre handed it to him, asking if he'd care to have it. With thanks the guard accepted the little gift, conscious of its unique historical value.*

---

*See below, 133.

The young artist hadn't used a mirror, later marveled Tomlinson, hadn't glanced at another picture for guidance. Yet the sketch looked just like him! Never did he suspect the truth, that over the years Andre had drawn, sketched, and painted so many portraits of himself that he could almost do it blindfolded.

PART TWO

IV

THE DAYS BEFORE — BLUNDER

F ully clothed except for his boots and his regimental tunic, Major John Andre lay stretched on a narrow bunk in a cramped, candlelit cabin aboard the *Vulture*. His eyes were closed but he wasn't sleeping. He was waiting, listening for the sound of visiters treading the deck overhead. At the moment only the occasional creak of the ship's planking could be heard as it drifted around its anchor cable on the ebb tide. It was September 22, 1780. The hour was just after midnight.

For several days Andre had been aboard the sloop, an armed vessel anchored in the Hudson near Haverstraw, some twenty miles below West Point. As he lay trying his best to relax, he couldn't keep from thinking over and over that the most important event of his life was at hand, a meeting with the famous American general, Benedict Arnold, commander at the Point. If all went as planned, then the rebellion of the American colonies, after dragging on for almost four years, would be finished within a matter of weeks, completely crushed. Only needed now was the secret meeting with General Arnold to settle the terms of his reward for the betrayal and to coordinate plans for the British attack on the Point's deliberately weakened fortifications. A couple of hours' conversation, then a swift return to New York City on the *Vulture*, and the next day the attack would be launched upriver. An hour or so of fighting, rolling up the American troops in position after position, should bring total surrender. Arnold would see that it didn't go on too long.

Andre smiled a satisfied little smile. To think that he—still six months from his thirtieth birthday, and a lowly major—was at the center of the prodigious scheme! He hadn't conceived it, hadn't initiated it, but at General Clinton's orders had responded to Arnold's initial feelers. Then for more than a year he'd deftly nudged the plot along. Promotion to brigadier-general would be the least of his reward. Elevation to the nobility was almost certain, a baronet, say, or quite possibly much higher, even a dukedom.

Some details about the meeting were still open, most importantly just where and just when it would take place (matters not easily arranged in a day of painfully slow communication and always uncertain transport, and in which both parties occupied highly visible positions. Already two previous tries had been missed when some little arrangement went awry). Whether Arnold meant to come aboard the *Vulture*, Andre wasn't sure. Possibly he'd be expected to go ashore. If so, it would have to be on neutral ground, for he had General Clinton's strict orders not to enter American lines, and by no means to change his uniform for civilian clothes. This wasn't so much to safeguard Andre as it was to ensure the success of the mission—*nothing* was to be done or attempted that might raise the least chance of failure. Andre had also been told that under no circumstances was he to carry incriminating documents. If he received vital information to carry back, he was to memorize it if possible, or he might write it in code on some innocuous piece of paper.

There was a knock at the cabin door. It opened and a head popped in, that of Colonel Beverly Robinson, an American Loyalist who from the first had been an adviser to the British on the plot.

Is he here? asked Andre, abruptly sitting up.

No, it's not General Arnold. He sent a man. You're to go with him. Arnold's waiting for you ashore.

Pulling on his boots and hastily shouldering into his tunic—a smartly tailored jacket of bright red with gold trim and green facings—Andre started to follow Robinson out.

Better put on an overcoat, Major, cautioned Robinson. Remember you're going as Mr. Anderson, a New York merchant.

Andre stopped, thought a moment, then asked what difference it made. He was going on shore under cover of night for an hour or two, would be on neutral ground, would meet no one but Arnold, and would be coming directly back to the ship. Why cover his uniform? He'd prefer to be completely open as to his true character, as General Clinton said he should.

Yes, but why risk it? Simple enough to wear an overcoat and be at ease. Another thing, we don't know much about the men who've been sent for you, whether they're in on the thing or not. Knowing how Arnold operates, they probably know only as much as is needed. I'll let you have a coat of mine.

Andre nodded agreement and the two went down the passageway to Robinson's cabin where Andre shrugged into a long, high-collared coat, in color a dark, purplish blue. Then Robinson led the way to the captain's cabin.

There were no handshakes, no formal introductions. Instead, as the *Vulture*'s skipper, Captain Sutherland, stood by, Robinson curtly indicated that Mr. Joshua Smith here—a nod toward Smith, who nodded in turn at Andre—was the personal emissary of the American general. He'd just arrived in a boat with two oarsmen, and had already explained that Arnold would be waiting on the beach at the foot of Long Clove Mountain. From the ship it was a row upriver of almost two miles, all of it against a strong ebb tide.* The rowboat was large and heavy, really a barge or lifeboat, and by rights ought

---

*The lower Hudson River, being for much of its length an arm of the sea, has regular tides. This fact and its bearing on the Andre story has escaped almost all previous writers. None dwells on it.

to be manned by four men. With only two men to buck the outgoing tide, the trip could take a half-hour or more. Best to get started.

To Smith he added, pointing, this is Mr. Anderson.

Andre, suddenly wary, asked, how do we know he's from Arnold?

Smith put his hand in his pocket and took out a small slip of paper which he handed to Andre. The few words scrawled in ink read simply, "Gustavus to Mr. Anderson."

I'm ready, said Andre, recognizing the pseudonym Arnold had used in his long correspondence with the British, and which was known to very few in English intelligence.

Leaving the cabin with the other three, Smith was struck by the evident fact of Andre's extreme youth, combined with a peculiarly polite address. "Mr. Anderson, from his youthful appearance and the softness of his manners," wrote Smith later in a brief description of his visit to the *Vulture*, "did not seem to me to be qualified for a business of such moment." That easy, unguarded reference to "a business of such moment" in that particular context, seems to show that Smith's knowledge of the plot was a good deal more complete than he later admitted.

Swung by the ebb tide around its anchor cable to the south, the *Vulture*'s slim, jutting prow was pointed north. This presented her port side to the western shore and to Smith's rowboat, which now rode alongside the sloop's dark, curving hull. In it sat two oarsmen, brothers who were tenants of Smith in Haverstraw, experienced rivermen named Sam and Joe Cahoon. As Smith and Andre climbed over the ship's side and down the rope ladder the brothers held the boat in close.

Nowhere on the rowboat could a flag of truce be seen. A white truce pennant had indeed been flying at its bow as it approached the *Vulture*, but had been taken down. Its purpose was temporary, meant to reassure the ship's watch that the rowboat wasn't hostile. For Andre's secret approach to a neutral, and in this case friendly shore, a flag of truce would have been superfluous. In addition, it seems, that

Andre was uncomfortable at the thought of using a flag when it wasn't needed and would convey no particular advantage. The stories that were sure to be told and retold about this momentous day he didn't want marred by the stigma of an unfair and unsoldierly action.

As Robinson warned, the trip to Long Clove proved to be a long, hard pull, lasting nearly an hour with no chance to rest without being carried back by the tide. Seated side by side in the ample stern, the two men spoke little, only, as Smith recalled, a few comments now and again about the hampering tide, the coolness of the night, and some other "matters of no concern." The two men in any case, strangers to each other, could have had little to discuss under those unique circumstances. Andre couldn't be sure how much Smith actually knew. Smith, knowing something of what was afoot and suspecting the rest (perhaps not the entire plot to surrender both West Point and Washington), wasn't sure he wanted to know more.

It was nearly two A.M. when the boat glided silently into the shallow water below the looming shadow of Long Clove Mountain. With the keel grinding up on the pebbly sand, Smith peered along the beach but could see no one. The general, he said, must be waiting among the trees a little way up the slope. Picking up a dark lantern he said he'd go and see. Two minutes later he was back. Yes, Arnold was up there concealed in a thick clump of firs.

As Andre picked his way up the hill among the trees, a thin stab of light hit his face. Major Andre? inquired a thick, gruff voice from behind the dark lantern.

Yes. General Arnold?

The thin beam swung around and shone on the holder's face, illuminating heavy, thick-lipped features with a sharply prominent nose. Yes, said the voice. We can sit over here on these rocks.

Here a veil falls over the scene, neither man having left any record of what the two talked about. If Andre had lived he surely would have written in graphic terms of that fateful night. Arnold did live, another twenty years, but uttered hardly a word. Still, while the details of the two-plus hours the plotters spent conferring in the shadows are lost to history, their main topics of concern are easily recovered.

At first the two soldiers, enemies until then, would have exchanged some remarks about the war, by that time almost five years in progress. This part of the conversation would have had some importance, for the American cause in the fall of 1780 had begun to totter—in the ranks disaffection and dissatisfaction, Congress crying out for nonexistent funds, separate states defying governmental authority, battles being lost or avoided, while regiments of trained British Regulars swarmed everywhere. Many Americans were joining in the anguished call for a negotiated peace in which the colonies, gaining some concessions, would resume their allegiance to the Crown. In such a situation, even aside from the military advantage, the fall of West Point would be sure to bring the rebellion to a crashing halt.

Gun by gun, fortification by fortification, the coming British attack on the Point was layed out between the two—how many men would be defending which positions, where the defenses were weakest, which ramparts could be quickly overwhelmed, where and how fires could be set to do the most damage to wooden redoubts and walls, how the heavier guns would mostly misfire, at what point in the one-sided battle Arnold would order a surrender. Integral to the plan was the capture of Washington himself. At a strategic moment during the attack, it was agreed, Arnold would send urgently to Washington at Tappan for reinforcements. The Commander-in-Chief himself would certainly lead his troops to the rescue, only to be intercepted by a British force lying in wait. With West Point in British hands and the peerless leader in custody or dead (either was acceptable to Arnold), despair would spread quickly in American ranks, civilian as well as military. By now there were few Americans who didn't understand that on George Washington's sturdy shoulders rested any remaining hope of victory.

Finishing their discussion of the military aspects, Arnold pulled a thick envelope from his pocket. There were too many details for anyone to remember correctly, or to commit to writing in code. These papers—he held the envelope toward Andre—contain all the needed information, everything we've just gone over and more.

Andrè shook his head. Can't take them, he said. I'm under orders to carry no papers.

Though surprised, Arnold didn't hesitate to insist. There's no risk, he urged. From there, Andre would be going right back to the ship. If it made him feel any better, if he was leery of running into a rebel guard boat (they hardly ever came down this far), he need only have the papers tied to a stone. Just drop them into the water.

It made sense, agreed Andre. Obviously, General Clinton hadn't taken the time to think through his order. Supposing he got back to New York and was asked a specific question by the tacticians about the fortifications that he couldn't answer! Then, too, weren't the papers in a way an earnest of Arnold's good faith? He took the envelope and shoved it into his breast pocket.

During the meeting or at its end, Arnold broached the subject closest to his heart, the sum to be paid him for his treason. In a general way they'd covered this in their earlier secret correspondence, now it was time to make firm commitments. For a successful turnover of West Point, with or without the capture of Washington, Arnold would receive the lump sum of 20,000 pounds, an enormous amount for the time, plus indemnification for loss of various properties. Also, he would take a place in the British army as a brigadier, one step below his American rank. If by some accident matters didn't turn out as planned, if West Point didn't wind up a British possession, he would be paid only half the principal sum, with property indemnification and the same brigadiership.

At first Andre hesitated. While the higher sum for a successful outcome had been approved by General Clinton, he explained, in case of failure he'd "been commissioned to promise only six thousand pounds sterling." There followed some earnest haggling on Arnold's part, which quickly led the wary Andre to agree. "He would use his influence," he promised, "and recommend it to [General Clinton] to allow the sum proposed," quickly adding that "he had no doubt that [Clinton] would accede to the higher sum." At this critical juncture Andre was taking no chances that the greedy traitor might turn troublesome and threaten to back out. (Of course Andre never saw General Clinton again, so the traitor pocketed only the original six thousand.)

A noise lower down the slope brought the talk to a halt, and Smith came into view. Did the general realize it was now nearly four o'clock and that daylight would soon be breaking? Mr. Anderson should be getting back to the ship if it was to be done by dark.

Arnold said all right, he was finished. Did Andre—Mr. Anderson—have anything more? No, he didn't. All three descended the hill to the beach.

Surprisingly no one had given any thought to the change of the tide. Arnold specially had made a grievous mistake in selecting the time and place of the meeting without checking the tides. Long Clove was upriver from the ship, so that in coming ashore the ebb tide had been against them. Now going back they'd have to struggle with a flood tide. The meeting place should have been downriver from the ship, a couple of miles below Long Clove. It was not until the Cahoon brothers grumpily complained about the hardship of rowing an undermanned big boat against a flood tide—much harder than in coming ashore since the ebb had been nearly slack—did anyone realize the error. Not on its face a major miscalculation, it quickly became the one egregious mistake that led to the doom of the entire enterprise.

The Cahoons knew the river, were aware of tide speeds and timing and when dawn would make their boat visible to all. From the start they hadn't liked the job Smith paid them to do. Such secret business as boarding an enemy ship at night and hidden meetings ashore struck both brothers as more than strange. At first Sam Cahoon had

refused the task, telling Smith that "he was afraid to go." Just as
leery, Joe Cahoon went on record more at length: "I asked him why
the flag [of truce] was not sent down in the daytime, as it ought to
be done. He said because it was to be kept private from the inhabitants and common men . . . I then told him I did not choose to go.
He said there was no hurt in going at all, and said if anything should
come against me, he would defend me and clear me from all. I told
him he could not clear me if there was anything bad in it." Against
Smith's insistent urging the brothers "stood out a great while before
we consented to go."

Now as Smith roused the brothers, who had dozed off in the boat
on the beach while waiting, their original reluctance grew into downright refusal. It was too late, they said flatly, now convinced that
something "bad" was taking place. Against a flood tide, especially
tired as they were, they'd be caught by full daylight before they were
halfway to the ship. They wouldn't go, they said, and staunchly held
out against all Smith's arguments and offers of added payment.

The curious, the revealing thing to note here is the silence of
Andre. It was in his interest to get safely back to the *Vulture* by the
shortest and quickest route possible. Yet in the face of the brothers'
refusal he said nothing, did nothing.

Coming ashore, as he testified at his trial, he'd supposedly been
told that if it became "too late to fetch me back," he would be hidden
ashore "until the next night in a place of safety." That simply wasn't,
couldn't be true. When the meeting was set up initially neither Arnold nor Andre would have expected or allowed for any needless
delay, certainly not risking a long stay on shore no matter how well
hidden, some sixteen hours or more. Neither had any reason to think
that their meeting might be protracted until it was "too late" to reach
the ship. What Andre claimed about a provision for waiting until
the next night to return was a convenient afterthought meant to
cover his dismal failure to take charge of his own destiny. If unable
to cajole or to threaten the brothers into making the trip, or by

offering more additional pay than they could refuse, he should simply have leveled a pistol at the two and ordered them to man the oars. They could have been held aboard the ship and released days later, after it was all over. Or not released, as it suited the British. In the larger scheme of things during those momentous hours the fate of two plain American civilians couldn't have meant much.

Of course Andre couldn't simply leap into the boat and make his own way. One man alone could never control so large a boat in a flood tide. But he might have hunted up a small skiff or towed a canoe along from the ship, and there was also his failure to arrange with the *Vulture*'s skipper for a return in an emergency. The skipper, Captain Sutherland, later was at some pains to deny any responsibility for the oversight. "Measures might have been concerted," he explained in some embarrassment to General Clinton, "for taking him off whenever he pleased, which he very well knew I at any time was enabled to accomplish." All too clearly it was Andre's inexperience, and his habitual desire to impress others by an easy, accommodating manner, that now robbed him of the ability to act with decision. At that moment of helplessness his important mission and, as it would turn out, his life were forfeit.

Almost equally at fault was Arnold, for when the Cahoons held back he didn't insist. With him, obviously, it was a case of overweening self-confidence, a belief, not unreasonable, that as Commander he enjoyed unlimited protection, could move the pieces of the game around at will. Perhaps feeling that there was more to be worked out with Andre, knowing that Smith's large house in Haverstraw was a bare half-hour away by horseback, he made his fateful decision. Smith he told to return the boat (a matter of going upriver along the shore *with* the tide), and said he'd take Andre to Haverstraw.

From Andre came no demur, no anxious questions as to the location of the Smith house in Haverstraw. British intelligence knew very well where the American lines were, knew that they ran east and west at Haverstraw. Riding north into the city from Long Clove Mountain, Andre would or should have understood that, in further bland disobedience of his orders, he'd be penetrating the American camp. Still he said nothing.

Two horses were waiting near the road further up the hill, Arnold's own and that of a negro servant who'd accompanied him. The servant could walk back, directed Arnold as he took the reins from the man and handed them to Andre. A ten-minute ride at a walk along the darkened road brought them to the edge of Haverstraw—where as Andre later claimed he "passed a guard I did not expect to see." On that same point in his letter to Washington he is more forthright and firm about his surprise at encountering the sentry. After a meeting "upon ground not within the posts of either army," he says he was told that

> the approach of day would prevent my return, and that I must be concealed until the next night. I was in my regimentals, and had fairly risked my person.
>
> Against my stipulation, my intention, and without my knowledge beforehand, I was conducted within one of your posts. Your Excellency may conceive my sensation on this occasion . . .

How that statement may have struck Washington isn't known, but its clever special pleading is now all too evident. He means, of course, that having gone *that* far, hearing the challenge of the American sentry, and knowing that a few more steps would carry him within rebel lines, he had no choice but to go on, had nowhere else to go, and so was "conducted" against his will inside American lines. The term is precisely the right one for its context and purpose. Roundly if subtly it declares that the fault wasn't his, that blame should rest on whoever "conducted" him, neatly avoiding the question of why he let himself be conducted, why when he heard the

Home of Joshua Smith in Haverstraw, where Andre was concealed before attempting his escape, accompanied by Smith. Locally it was called "Treason House." Below: sketch made in 1850 of the view from an upper window of the Smith house, looking toward the Hudson River where lay the Vulture. From Lossing, Field Book, 753.

sentry he didn't stop and go back the other way, why he didn't insist on being taken to a place outside the lines.

Through Haverstraw's unpaved streets, while the sky grew steadily brighter, for another mile or so the two horses plodded. High on a hillside, overlooking the city and the river beyond, sat Smith's large, square, two-story stone-and-stucco house. At the wide steps of the spacious porch the two turned in and dismounted. As Arnold led the horses round to the back of the building and tethered them, Andre went inside.

TELLER'S POINT IS A LARGE, sharp jut of land extending into the Hudson from the eastern shore and marking the lower end of Haverstraw Bay. The Point itself lies a mile or so further south than Long Clove Mountain, opposite. Off Teller's Point, about a half-mile distant, lay the *Vulture*. Here, about five A.M. on the morning of September 22, as Andre and Arnold sat eating breakfast at the Smith house, there occurred one of those unexpected incidents in the tale of Arnold's treachery that led people to talk of "the interposition of Providence" and the hand of God.

Entirely on his own, an American officer commanding that part of the shoreline brought cannon-fire to bear on the ship, driving it from its mooring and back downriver.

Colonel James Livingston, at age thirty-two an experienced combat officer, was headquartered at Verplanck's Point, ten miles north of Teller's Point. For a week he'd been hearing complaints from the Americans living along the shore about having an enemy ship sit unmolested so close to them. The possibility of a quick strike by a landing party from the ship to gain supplies or do incidental damage bothered and annoyed everyone, not to mention the patriotic resentment all felt at having the hated British flag flying so near and so boldly. No rebel vessels were available in the river to challenge and chase it off, so there it sat growing more of an irritation by the hour. *What* in the first place, people demanded to know, was it *doing* there? Colonel Livingston, it developed, felt the very same way, and he had the means of doing something about it.

The day before, the twenty-first, not bothering to ask permission of his superiors at West Point, Livingston ordered three field pieces—two small cannon throwing solid shot and a howitzer throwing shells—taken down to the extreme tip of the Point. The location was not a military installation but a more or less open stretch of land having only two or three private dwellings, widely spaced. Expecting that the ship would reply with her own guns to an attack from shore, Livingston had some earthworks built up, enough to protect guns and gunners.

Soon after first light on September 22, somewhere between five and five-thirty, the three guns began firing. He would, determined Livingston, at least drive the offending ship downriver, back toward its own lines.

Colonel Beverly Robinson, still waiting aboard the *Vulture* for Andre's return, and growing ever more apprehensive when nothing was heard, in a letter to Clinton explains what happened next:

> . . . on Thursday night they brought down on Tallers Point one six pdr and a howitzer, intrenched themselves on the very Point and at daybreak Fryday morning began a very hot fire on us from both which continued two hours, and would have been longer but luckily their magazine blew up.
>
> It was near high water the tide very slack and no wind, so that it was impossible, tho' every exertion was made, to get the ship out of their reach sooner. Six shot hulled us, one between wind & water, many others struck the sails, rigging, and boats on deck. Two shells hit us one fell on the Quar. deck another near the main shrouds. Capt. Sutherland is the only person hurt & he very slightly on the nose by a splinter.
>
> Capt. Sutherland has wrote to Sir. George Rodney desiring to have a galley or some other reinforcement if it should be

necessary for us to continue here any time longer . . . I shall do everything in my power to come at some knowledge of Mjr Andre . . .

The ship's log tells more, including the fact that the pounding even by small guns wasn't taken lightly, returning fire in addition to making a frantic effort to tow the vessel out of range, where its own bigger guns could still hit their target:

> . . . at 5 the Rebels opened a battery on us at Tallers Point, and began a heavy cannonade with shot and shell, which we returned—at ½ past 5 weighed [anchor]. Got the boats ahead and towed out—at ½ past six we silenced their fire . . . We received six shots in the hull (one of which was between wind and water) and three through the boats on the booms—the standing and running rigging shot away in many different places—two of the iron stantions broke by their shot. Several of their shells broke [exploded] over us and many of the pieces dropt on Board.

A record kept by the ship's sailing master agrees on the damage done, but gives different times: "At half past five A.M. the Rebels began a heavy cannonade on us from Taller's Point with shott and shells—weighed [anchor] and returned their fire—at eight came to with the best bower [anchor] in 4 fathoms."

Towing a sloop by two auxiliary boats, even in slack tide and with twenty or thirty men hauling on the oars, couldn't have been easy. While preparations for the towing were hurriedly being made, the ship's eight-gun broadside was unleashed against the makeshift rebel battery, and at least one direct hit was scored on a powder magazine. Then its guns fell silent as the ship was pulled around by the boats and it began slowly receding from Teller's Point, the rebel shot and shell still raining down as it went. The effective range of Livingston's small guns was perhaps a mile or a bit more, so very shortly the ship would have been out of reach.

How far downriver the *Vulture* was pulled neither skipper nor master records, but Robinson's letter gives the needed information. It is headed, "Vulture off Sinsink." This was the present Sing Sing, at the city of Ossining, two miles below Teller's Point. Though making the ship harder to reach by rowboat, the actual distance didn't matter too much. The important thing was that with the change of position it could no longer be seen from the Smith house in Haverstraw.

V

THE DAYS BEFORE — FLIGHT

Pushing open the large front door of the Smith house, Andre stepped into the paneled foyer where he waited for Arnold. At the moment only a lone servant was on hand, who didn't hear the two men enter and never saw Andre. Smith's wife and children had gone to visit relatives further north at Fishkill. Their absence at the time was not planned but was coincidence, though Arnold had learned of it earlier. Had the family been present in the house he still wouldn't have hesitated to take Andre there for concealment overnight. If the plot had succeeded—none of those involved thought there was the least chance of anything going really wrong— in the space of a few days the whole area for miles above and below West Point and on both sides of the river would have become British territory, including Haverstraw. By then it wouldn't have mattered much who knew what.

Arnold, who had many times been a guest in the house, led the way upstairs to a spacious sitting room at the building's front. Two large windows gave a magnificent view down to the river and far across to the Westchester hills, rising a misty blue in the distance.

Entering, Andre stopped for a look out one of the windows, his eyes searching along the river for the *Vulture*. There it lay, just visible past a headland on the near shore, hardly more than a black dot on the shimmering surface some eight miles away. With a heavy sigh he calculated the hours until darkness fell and he could make his way aboard: at least fifteen, more if there were any difficulty about getting a boat and men to row it.

Standing beside him at the window, Arnold caught the anxious air and said not to worry. He'd be back among his friends in no time. Nothing now could interfere with their plans. The marvelous coup, so long in prospect, was almost accomplished. The beginning of the end for American independence was at hand. Meantime they could go over some fine points of the weakened defenses at West Point, how he would disperse his troops, fragmenting them over the hills and in exposed pockets. Not only would the king gain strategic West Point, there would also be some three thousand prisoners to be taken—the core of Washington's army!—along with a huge pile of ammunition and other stores.

A dull, far-off booming came through the closed windows of the sitting room as the two men conferred at a table. Both looked up. To them the sound of cannon, near or far, muffled or not, was a familiar one. Arnold especially reacted in alarm. He knew of no planned action at that time and place that called for the use of artillery. Had there been some sort of surprise attack by the British? Jumping to his feet, Arnold hurried to a window, followed by the equally anxious Andre. Both men instantly spotted the source of the firing.

In the air around and over the *Vulture* drifted large, ragged wisps and puffs of smoke. Hovering over Teller's Point could be seen a similar pattern. The ship was trading fire with a shore battery! Was it under attack, had the rebel battery for some reasoned started it? Or had the ship opened fire first? Perplexed, the two continued to watch and before long had the answer. The ship's longboats were being deployed, obviously in an attempt to pull her off, out of range of the rebel guns. The foresail had also been let fly, but it hung there lifeless showing not a ruffle of wind.

Only for a fleeting moment did either man ask himself *why* the strange action had erupted. It was enough to see its worrying result, in fact that the ship was about to drop some distance downriver. As they watched, neither spoke but both had the same anxious thought: *how far will it go?*

The process of getting the ship moving behind the longboats' towlines was an agonizingly slow one, but at last it was turned and gliding ponderously, the lone sail still hanging limp. Foot by foot it moved as the two men at the window watched, hoping it would halt after having gone what seemed a mile. It didn't. The limp sail suddenly came to life, partially filling as a light wind gusted. The towlines were cast off, another long stretch was covered—and the ship disappeared from sight, the view from Smith's window cut off by the bulge of land at the foot of High Tor Mountain.

Andre's heart sank and he looked over at Arnold. A bare four hours ago as he climbed over the ship's side it had all seemed so simple, so sure, so unstoppable! A meeting ashore, then a fast return to the ship, and that was it. Now what? Of course if he was unable to get back to the *Vulture*, he could still reach New York City by land, but it would take more time and involve greater danger. Still, maybe the *Vulture* hadn't dropped down too far.

Can you send someone to find where she stopped? he asked Arnold eagerly, a sudden look of hope on his face.

Yes, replied Arnold, but it's not the distance that worries me. An incident like that stays alive for a while. Guard boats and telescopes from shore will be watching night and day to see where she goes, what she does. Even if she comes back up a way, it's not the same. Might be best for you to go back by land.

Andre shook his head in a vigorous *no*.

Don't worry, it'll be all right. I'll give you a pass. It'll take you safely across the river and down through our lines to the Neutral Ground, and then it's an easy couple of hours to New York. Smith'll go with you.

There was a pause before Arnold added, of course you can't go in that uniform. You'll have to put on civilian clothes. You and Smith are about of a size. He'll let you have what's needed.

Andre had removed his overcoat and now stood there in his full scarlet regalia. At Arnold's mention of civilian dress he threw up his hands and again shook his head. No, no, General, I can't. My orders from General Clinton forbid it. Besides, you know that the instant I make the switch, here inside your lines, I will become a spy, legally and in fact a spy. That's not a role I care to fill.

The sour look on Andre's face showed the utter distaste he felt at the thought of appearing as such a despised character, so far beneath the consideration of a gentleman. No, he would not under any circumstances doff his regimental tunic. If he had to go by land he'd wear his overcoat. A risk, but he'd do it.

For some seconds before answering, Arnold stared at his youthful cohort. Major, he said finally, as a man of honor the sentiment does you credit. But it's really a bit short-sighted, a bit selfish, if I may say that. You're willing to put in jeopardy our whole operation, which could end the war, saving many lives and much blood, just to suit the niceties of your personal tastes! Major, we're talking of using ordinary clothes for only a few brief hours, long enough to get you from here to the Neutral Ground, a matter of a few miles. Once you're *there* it won't matter *what* you've got on!

Another pause and he added, Major, wearing a unform like that, even covered up by a coat, as you pass our different sentries and posts and encampments makes no sense at all. Accidents happen, the overcoat is no guarantee . . . Major, I'm not suggesting you become an actual spy. I know you'd never do that. This is just to get you out of a tight spot. An operation of this magnitude calls for a readiness to improvise . . .

No, sir, it's out of the question, came back Andre, his lips tightened in grim refusal.

A step sounded on the stair and both men turned to the door, Andre reaching hastily to don his overcoat. The door opened and in shambled Joshua Smith, stooped and looking tired and bedraggled from his night's exertion. He knew all about the trouble with the *Vulture*, so wasn't surprised to hear Arnold ask about a land return for Andre.

Going by land, he answered, might in fact be the safer route, now that attention was fixed on the ship. It was a longer way, yet in the end could prove even faster than going by water, what with getting hold of a boat again and willing rowers and not forgetting the uncertainties of wind and tide.

Andre still held back. I'm sure the *Vulture* will manage to come up again, he grumbled. Who'd spot us in the dark?

Dropping the pretense about "Mr. Anderson," to Smith Arnold said that if they did go by land the major would need to change his uniform. Did Smith have some clothes he could lend, say a shirt, stock, vest, jacket, and hat? Andre could keep his own britches and boots.

To this point Andre had been uncertain how much Smith knew of the plot and whether he should allow the man to see him in uniform. At Arnold's words he pulled off the overcoat and threw it on a chair. Smith glanced at the red tunic but showed no sign of surprise. (At his own trial later Smith would claim to have been *very* surprised by this revelation of the British agent's true identity, but had accepted Arnold's assertion that the tunic had been "borrowed" by Mr. Anderson from an officer friend and worn out of vanity. Few believed him then. Now almost no one does.)

Clothes would be no trouble, said Smith looking at Andre, who was again vigorously shaking his head, but saying nothing.

General, went on Smith, whichever way we go we'll need passes. Certainly for the land route. But with the guard boats stirred up it'll be good to have one for water travel, even at night and just in case. Nodding, Arnold sat down at a desk, took pen and paper, and wrote:

> Joshua Smith has permission to pass with a boat and three hands and a flag to Dobb's Ferry, on public business, and to return immediately.

That would take care of the water route, the reference to Dobbs Ferry being a blind. Smith would go only as far as the *Vulture*, wherever it lay. Again he took his quill pen and wrote, this time scribbling out two passes:

> Permit Mr. John Anderson to pass the guards to the White Plains or below, if he chuses. He being on public business by my direction.

> Joshua Smith has permission to pass the guards to the White Plains and to return, he being on public business by my direction.

All three passes he dated September 22 from "Headquarters," signing them. "B. Arnold, M. Gen." Why for the land route he separated the two isn't clear. It may simply have been protocol at the time. Or it may have been done at Smith's request, allowing him at a certain juncture to turn back, wherever he judged that it was safe for Andre to go on alone.

Arnold stood up and reached for his hat. He had to get back to headquarters, he explained, handing over the three passes. The decision as to which route would be taken he'd leave to the two men involved to make. One seemed as good as the other. Either way, with the passes, nothing could go wrong.

"From this time," recalled Smith in describing Andre's mood in the hours after Arnold's departure, "he seemed shy, and desirous to avoid much conversation; he continued to urge preparations for his departure, and carefully avoided being seen by persons that came to the house."

Atop the wide, gently sloping roof of the building stood a typical widow's walk. It gave a magnificently sweeping view of the countryside for many miles in every direction, but particularly to the east and the four-mile-wide expanse of the river at Haverstraw Bay. In the afternoon, to provide the brooding Andre with some brief distraction during his long hours of waiting, Smith invited him to the roof to enjoy the unusual view—countryside that in only a few short days would no longer be rebel territory, but British.

It wasn't the sight of rolling hills and shimmering water that interested Andre, it was the chance to see a little further down the river past High Tor, possibly spotting the truant ship. Standing with Smith on the windy walkway, he looked longingly in the direction of the vessel—still nowhere to be seen—"and with a heavy sigh wished he was on board."

ANDRE'S MOST CONSPICUOUS PERSONALITY trait was his peculiar ability to make an instant favorable impression on all whom he met even briefly, an impression in which the presence of exceptional talents was strongly hinted. It had earned him, with breathtaking speed, military preferment. The irony is that it also brought about his downfall. No man could have been less qualified than Andre to act the part of a secret agent, or even a clandestine go-between. He'd been handed the assignment by General Clinton only because of that curious knack he had of making people believe he'd be equal to *any* undertaking. At the Smith house on the afternoon of September 22 he again demonstrated just how wrong that belief could be. This time his stumbling cost him his life.

Left on record by Andre are three statements as to why he changed out of his uniform. All three say something different, and none provides the true reason for the fatal action.

First is the claim made in his letter to Washington in which he reveals his identity. He was, he says, taken inside American lines against his wishes: "Thus become a prisoner, I had to concert my escape. I quitted my uniform, was passed another way in the night without the American posts . . ." Of course he was not a prisoner, not in any sense, and he had no need to "escape." At any time he could have insisted to Arnold that he be conducted outside American lines the same way he'd entered. For that, with a pass, he needn't have quitted his uniform, or gone by night.

Second was his statement to General Clinton, made to assure his Commander that the difficulty in which he found himself was *neither* his own fault nor the general's:

> ... the events of coming within an enemy's posts, and of changing my dress, which led me to my present situation, were contrary to my own intentions, as they were to your orders ...

The act of changing his dress, he says, was done "contrary" to his intent. This seems the opposite of saying that he did it to "concert" or facilitate his "escape." How he was forced to do something so crucial yet against his intention, he doesn't say.

The third mention occurs in the statement he read to the Court of Inquiry. Coming at the statement's close, it strikes a reader almost as a trivial afterthought: "I have omitted mentioning that, when I found myself within an enemy's posts, I changed my dress." Now the reason he gives for the change is simply that he "found" himself to be inside American lines, as if he couldn't understand how he got there, so that ridding himself of his uniform was the only sensible thing to do (something that any well-trained officer in a similar fix on either side might do, he subtly implies).

Of course none of the three explanations was haphazard. All three waltz deftly around the undeniable fact that he *did* discard his uniform while minimizing the fact as much as possible. The real explanation he knew very well, but consciously avoided. He changed his uniform because, unable to make the decision himself, he allowed Smith to decide on the return route. Smith chose to go by land—a circuitous, forty-mile journey fraught with danger despite Arnold's safe-conduct passes—which made the wearing of a uniform, even covered by an overcoat, appear ridiculous.

Andre's ultimate agreement to the plan didn't come without argument, half-hearted as it was. When the idea of a land return was first broached, he "objected much against it, and thought it was settled that in the way I came I was also to return." But toward evening he gave in, his reason being that Smith "to my great mortification persisted in his determination of carrying me by the other route." It was also Smith's "persistence" which finally got Andre to leave off his uniform and try on some of Smith's own shirts, vests, and jackets. All felt a little snug, even on the slender Andre, but one bluish jacket with gold-trimmed buttonholes did nicely. The hat was a plain black bowler-type with a wide, circular brim.

The term Andre uses to portray Smith's manner in the argument—"persistence"—in truth is only a self-deluding way of masking his own shocking incompetence. In the same way, "mortification" in that context simply disguises his complete if reluctant surrender to circumstances, *none* of which at that moment was beyond his control.

HOLDING HIS MUSKET at the ready across his chest, the American sentry challenged the two civilians on horseback as they turned in at the ferry entrance. Each leaned down to show his pass, but the guard gave them no more than a glance. He'd seen hundreds like them, all signed by the commander at West Point, General Arnold. He waved the two men on.

King's Ferry, three miles to the north of Smith's house, was the main Hudson River crossing. Just under a mile from shore to shore, it linked Stony Point on the western side and Verplanck's Point on the eastern. Now in full control of the rebel army, its barges and flatboats ran a regular service, and during the daylight hours it was in steady use. Beginning at dusk the traffic fell off, which is why Smith chose that time to arrive with his companion.

The two men walked their horses down the path toward the dock and as they came abreast of the ferry pavilion Smith turned aside to go in. He'd say hello to some friends, he explained, and they'd have a drink while waiting. Andre, wary of meeting anyone he didn't have to, his mood greatly subdued, said he'd go on and wait at the dock. Smith went in.

Now facing Andre, as Smith had explained the itinerary before leaving Haverstraw, were some four hours of journeying: the ferry ride, then a wide swing of ten or so miles heading a little north from the ferry landing to Peekskill, then again east and south another five miles, part of the time at a canter, most walking. They'd stop for the night at the home of some people he knew. After a few hours sleep they'd be on their way again at dawn. The Croton River was the dividing line, its far bank being the start of the Neutral Ground. At a place on the river called Pine's Bridge, Smith would turn back, leaving Andre to go the last fifteen miles on his own. From the bridge it was all open country, marked only by an occasional farm or private dwelling.

If he was stopped in the Neutral Ground by anyone at any time he need only show his pass and he'd be safe no matter who his accosters were, Rebels or Loyalists. Rebels would honor the pass and let him go on unmolested. Loyalists would ignore the pass and hold him for the English authorities, which would suit him even better. If stopped he need explain nothing, *just show his pass.*

It was those first fifteen or so miles, getting through the American lines, that might prove ticklish, Smith warned, a fact that was demonstrated before the two had gone half the distance.

Coming off the ferry at Verplank's Point, they guided their horses on the road up to and then past Peekskill, all without incident. By nine it was dark, and as they passed a long wooded section called Crompond, they unexpectedly found themselves surrounded by armed soldiers materializing out of the shadows. "Friends! Friends!" instantly called out Smith.

An officer strode up. Who are you? he asked. Where bound? Smith, leaning down to hand over his pass, explained that they were on special business for General Arnold. The officer—Ebenezer Boyd, captain of a militia patrol—took Smith's pass, also that of Andre, and told both men to dismount. Then he turned and led the way to

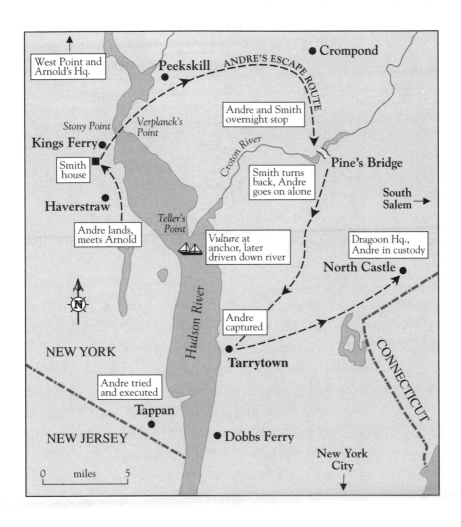

a shack hidden among the trees. Wait out here, he directed as he entered, adding that he needed a light to read the passes.

Andre's nerves began to tighten. Was the officer suspicious of them for some reason, was he playing for time? "On approaching the house," recalled Smith, "Mr. Anderson seemed very uneasy; but I cheered him by saying that our papers [the passes] would carry us to any part of the country . . . and that no person dare presume to detain us."

Captain Boyd, however, emerging from the building, did presume to detain the two, and for an anxious fifteen minutes or so. Obviously he was a man of independent mind, an experienced officer who knew that passes could be faked. The passes seemed in order, he said. But why were Mr. Smith and Mr. Anderson traveling so late? Where had they come from? Exactly where were they going? What was their business?

Smith answered all Boyd's questions straightforwardly, though in explaining their "business" he said only that it concerned the gathering of intelligence from certain parties near the city. They didn't mean to go all the way that night but would be stopping a few miles further on.

Boyd glanced at the two for a moment longer, then abruptly his manner changed to one of friendly concern. Going on further just then would be chancy, he warned. He'd heard that a band of troublemakers, maybe Skinners, maybe Cowboys, was raising a little hell in the countryside just below. A while ago he thought he'd heard some firing. If the two wanted to be safe they could go back a couple of miles to a place he knew, the farm of a friend named Andreas Miller. Mention his name and Miller would put them up for the night.

Andre's discomfort increased sharply. The captain's offer sounded to him like a subterfuge, a ploy meant to keep them in the vicinity while he did some checking. Bending close to Smith's ear he mumbled that he thought they should keep going, take the chance. Retracing their steps for a whole two miles didn't feel right.

Smith shook his head. To Boyd he said, thanks, Captain, thanks. We'll do that. He climbed into the saddle, waited as Andre mounted, then led the way back along the road they'd just come, "and my companion reluctantly followed."

Evidently trusting souls, the Millers, husband and wife, when they heard Boyd's name mentioned by the two strangers at their door, promptly invited them in. One large bed in a separate room was all they had available. Would that do? It would. On it Andre threw himself fully clothed, not removing either boots or spurs. If anything happened, he wasn't going to be taken at a disadvantage. Smith before lying down took the time to strip to his pants, undershirt, and socks.

Neither slept well, Andre apparently not at all. Then with the first streaks of dawn he was on his feet, pressing Smith to get up. Smith's later record of those slow, uncomfortable seven or so hours unwittingly captures the turmoil of apprehension that stirred Andre's spirit:

> . . . we slept in the same bed; and I was often disturbed with the restless motions and uneasiness of mind exhibited by my bed-fellow, who on observing the first approach of day, summoned my servant to prepare the horses for our departure.* He appeared in the morning as if he had not slept an hour during the night; he at first was much dejected, but a pleasing change took place in his countenance when summoned to mount his horse. The landlord, who was a very kind and civil man . . . refused to take any compensation for the trouble which we had given him.

Pleasant, Andre's handsome countenance may have been when starting out in the mists of morning that September 23, a Saturday. But it was twice roiled by understandable fear in two separate incidents, in one of which, as he himself confessed, "his hair stood erect and his heart was in his mouth."

Less than a half-hour along the road the two were again stopped

---

*A young negro servant of Smith's accompanied the two all the way from Haverstraw. Only here is he mentioned.

by a rebel sentry and an officer was called who asked for identification. The passes were produced, and after some desultory conversation about conditions in the area, the two were allowed to proceed.

The second incident, a little while later, involved a lone rider coming toward them on the road from the south. As the rider got closer both Smith and Andre could see that it was an American officer, but Andre saw more than that. With a shock he recognized Colonel Sam Webb, who while a prisoner of the English, Andre had gotten to know well and to like. They hadn't seen each other in a while, yet there was no doubt that Webb would know Andre on sight.

Wildly looking about for a way to avoid the meeting, Andre could think of nothing. The road was straight, only trees and open space on either side, and they were rapidly closing on each other.

Pulling his hat down on his eyes, Andre hunched his shoulders and hiked the coat collar up around his ears. Scarcely breathing, he lowered his head and fixed his eyes on the moving ground.

As they came abreast "the Colonel stared at him, but they kept moving and soon passed each other." His hair stirring, swallowing hard to clear his throat, Andre let out a long sigh and slumped in the saddle.

Minutes later his mood changed, swinging all the way to the opposite extreme as he "thought himself now past all danger." Glibly, voluminously, almost giddily, he began talking, racing from subject to subject. Smith describes the rush of talk he listened to from his suddenly exuberant companion as they went along the remaining miles to the river crossing at Pines Bridge:

> . . . his countenance brightened into a cheerful serenity, and he
> became very affable; in short I now found him highly enter-
> taining. He was not only well informed in general history, but
> well acquainted with that of America . . . he conversed freely
> on the belles lettres: music, painting, and poetry, seemed to be
> his delight. He displayed a judicious taste in the authors he

had read, possessed great elegance of sentiment, and a most pleasing manner of conveying his ideas, by adopting the flowery colouring of poetical imagery, [and] descanted on the richness of the scenery around us . . .

The pleasantry of converse, and mildness of the weather, so insensibly beguiled the time, that we at length found ourselves at the bridge before I thought we had got half the way; and I now had reason to think my fellow-traveler a different person from the character I had first formed of him . . .

With the bridge in sight they stopped at a small house and inquired if they could buy some breakfast. Answering the door was "an old matronly Dutch woman" who said apologetically that she had little food on hand to give, only a little cornmeal mush. Bowls of steaming mush in hand, the two sat on the back steps of the house and "made a good meal, our appetites being keen from having been supperless the preceding night."

(Was a stop at this juncture for such a reason really necessary, all things considered? But the famished Andre, thinking himself "past all danger," sat contentedly down with his own bowl of mush, when he should have left Smith to his meal and gone riding off.)

At the bridge Andre said he was without money and might need some before reaching his friends. Could Smith lend him a bit? Readily Smith handed over half of what he fished from his pocket. Then he repeated the directions he'd previously given Andre about the route to be followed, and with a warm handshake the two parted. At the last minute Andre pulled out his gold watch and pressed it on Smith as a reward for his efforts and a keepsake. With thanks Smith refused.

His mood still buoyant, now sure that by noontime he'd be standing in General Clinton's office making his report to a beaming superior, Andre waved a last goodbye and spurred his mount over the wooden bridge spanning the Croton River.

It wasn't money and gold watches that Andre should have been thinking about at that fateful parting. What he needed and should have had for the last leg of his journey as a solitary traveler, what he should have brought with him on leaving the *Vulture*, or failing that should have gotten from Arnold, was a gun, a pistol he could conceal under his overcoat. No secret agent of any sense or experience would have ventured into or tried to cross Westchester's turbulent Neutral Ground unarmed.

VI

THE DAYS BEFORE — CAPTURE

A husky six-footer, John Paulding at age twenty-two was already a veteran both of combat and of British prisoner-of-war camps. Twice he'd been captured while in action, and twice he'd escaped, on each occasion hurrying back to his outfit, the First Westchester Volunteer Militia.

His latest escape, a classic of soldierly daring, had taken place only the week before, in mid-September. As a sergeant in the militia company of Lieutenant Dan Peacock he'd been on patrol north of Tarrytown when the company was surprised by a troop of British regulars making a foray from the city. Outnumbered five to one in the fierce if brief fight that followed, the rebels sustained high casualties including a half-dozen killed. With twenty others, Paulding was taken prisoner and quickly herded back down to the city where at Manhattan's lower end he was placed with hundreds more in a walled compound. It took him some weeks to plan his escape but by mid-September he was ready.

Involved was the scaling of a high wooden fence at just the right location near a private dwelling that abutted on the prison. The negro maid from this house frequently came to the prison selling fruit to the inmates, and Paulding gambled on her willingness to help him.

While the prisoners were taking exercise in the yard one morning, some other inmates created a diversion. The two Hessian guards rushed to quell the disturbance, and while their backs were turned Paulding leaped onto a box he'd placed by the wall, jumped as high as he could, and managed to catch the wall's top edge. In a second he was over, dropping to the ground and making a short dash for the cellar of the house. Inside he found the maid who, recovering from her surprise, agreed to hide him for the night. In the prison he was soon missed and a search party was sent out to hunt him through the streets.

The following night he made his way uptown to the home of a friend he'd known in peacetime, who "furnished him with provisions, after secreting him for the night, and purchased for him a British uniform (a Jaeger coat, green, laced with red) in which to effect his escape from the city."

Next day in the guise of a British soldier, in broad daylight he walked north to the Bloomingdale section of Manhattan, then veered over to the Hudson shore looking for an unguarded rowboat. Spotting one tied to a deserted wharf, he waited until dark then crept down to the wharf, stole the boat, and rowed across the river, heading slightly up to avoid any British encampments. Landing, he found a road and trudged north until he was challenged by an American sentry. Within minutes he was inside a rebel post, standing in the office of General LaFayette himself, who questioned him closely about conditions among the enemy in the city. Next morning he was on his way back to Westchester.

Welcomed by his captain and his old comrades at the militia's South Salem headquarters, he was offered time to rest up from his adventure. He took only four days. Hearing that a special patrol was being formed to watch the roads leading into the city, he promptly volunteered.

The military situation in the Neutral Ground was a volatile one, confusing and always unpredictable, control of large parts of it shifting between the two foes and their sympathizers. Many sections of it had been left devastated, the victim of American and British raiding parties, along with the more random pillaging and marauding of the two less organized groups popularly styled Cowboys and Skinners (adherents of either the English or the Americans). Many old residents had been forced to flee, leaving homes and farms virtually empty, crops spoiling and cattle dying or stolen.

Especially important to the American cause was the interdiction of food and other supplies bound for the large British force in New York City. Cattle, including cows, in particular were subject to confiscation if it were suspected or proved that a herd on the road was intended for British use. Specific laws had been passed by federal and state authorities governing what and who could be allowed to pass the lines, and under what conditions.

In order to stimulate greater vigilance, the laws awarded to the soldiers themselves whatever contraband was intercepted, or the equivalent in money, as well as whatever valuables might be found on anyone attempting to pass the lines unlawfully. In enforcing these laws the militia was expected to be especially active, and this extended to militiamen who while excused from regular duty chose to take part. The rebel army itself had issued similar orders, insisting that all militia units keep scouting parties "continually patrolling down River and towards Croton to make Discoveries and to take any Scouts from the enemy and to kill all Tory villains found in arms against their country or plundering or carrying any Cattle or Goods to the enemy."

The little patrol that on September 23 banded together to watch the road leading to Tarrytown—on the Hudson shore some eight miles below Teller's Point—was made up of seven of these "off-duty" militiamen. As required, their leader, Sergeant John Yerkes, had obtained official permission for the action from an officer of the regular Continental army.

In taking up their position, the seven split into two smaller squads.

Four of the men stationed themselves on higher ground to the east. Sergeant Paulding and two privates were placed by the roadside among some trees where a narrow creek crossed the road, a half-mile out of Tarrytown. As usual, especially for the morning, traffic on the road was light, two or three wagons or horsemen passing in the first hour, all of whom were stopped, questioned, and allowed to continue. Positioned where they could watch a good stretch of the road from hiding, the three spent the time between challenges with a game of cards.

Paulding's two companions, also young, were hardened, battle-tested militiamen. David Williams, twenty-five, had been in the ranks for more than four years, since he took part in the siege of Quebec under General Montgomery. The third man, Isaac Van Wart, twenty, had already put in two years with the Westchester militia. Unlike Paulding, neither had spent any time in British prisoner-of-war camps.

As with the militia generally, none of the three wore a standard military uniform. Van Wart and Williams had on ordinary civilian clothes more or less alike—brown tunics, nondescript knee-britches, stockings, and cocked hats. Paulding, on the other hand, stood out as rather different in appearance. Conspicuously, he was still wearing the dark green, red-trimmed Jaeger uniform coat in which he'd made his escape from New York City. Why he hadn't bothered to change back to his own clothes is a question never asked of him, and for which he apparently never volunteered an answer, nor has anyone since thought to ask it.

Paulding wore the Jaeger uniform coat (standard issue in certain units of the Hessian mercenaries) because he thought it might give him and his squad an advantage. Posted somewhat near the British lines as they were, if necessary in a particular case, they could pose as Tories, British sympathizers, throwing any potential targets off guard. The Jaeger uniform would enhance that impression, though Paulding could whenever he wished simply take it off if he felt it wasn't needed or might prove awkward, appearing in ordinary shirt and vest. His wearing the Jaeger coat could not have been accidental or a mere happenstance, as writers and commentators always assume. In that particular situation the wearing of a British uniform *could* have been a real danger, at any moment proving a handicap rather than an advantage, a fact which Paulding would have known very well. He wore the jacket on purpose, and that purpose could only have been the one suggested here.

One of the sad oversights in the Andre story is the failure of professional historians and journalists to get more fully on record the detailed personal memories of these three men (each did leave a brief account of the capture). Part of the reason for the failure was the way they were regarded in earlier times, before the democratic spirit had taken hold in all levels of society. "Sturdy yeomen," they were often called, or in Alexander Hamilton's studied phrase, "simple peasants, leaning only on their own virtue and sense of duty."

Farmers, he might have said, not peasants, simple or otherwise. Uneducated is what he meant, drawing a stark contrast to the elegant, accomplished, very well educated, and decidedly not simple Major John Andre, Adjutant-General to the British Army.

ALMOST AS IF HIS HORSE were placidly treading the manicured bridle paths of London's Hyde Park, Andre sat contentedly in the saddle admiring the passing scenery. "A beautiful region of forest-clad hills," Washington Irving called it, "fertile valleys and abundant streams," though here and there showing the scars of war, "fields lying waste, the roads grass-grown, the country mournful, solitary, silent." The area through which Andre now rode showed fewer of these ravages than elsewhere. Many farms were still intact and being worked, many houses still comfortably held their original families.

Calm, even serene in spirit as he jogged along, Andre couldn't keep from thinking over and over how well it had all turned out for him, how very well everything had turned out.

How fortunate to have been here in America, at just the right time and in just the right place, so that he became the prime mover in the incredible treason of the great American general!

A year and a half of wishing, hoping, planning, of carefully maneuvering Benedict Arnold into asking for the West Point command so that he could betray it. Now, very soon it would be all over—two or three days!—the Yankee rebellion crushed, the colonies again dutiful subjects of the Crown.

He'd be the prime beneficiary of the triumph. Of that there was no doubt. Always since he was a young boy he'd felt that he was somehow larger than life, that he was destined to play a prominent role in—*what* he didn't know precisely, but something big, grand, something that would catch the attention of the world. He knew *that* much even as he toiled away at a desk in his father's counting house in London, hating every second of it and dreaming of parades, martial music, and that bright red uniform. Now he knew what it was, knew what would catapult him to the top. A dukedom might be the least of it. All through his short life he'd been looked on as a favorite by people in high places, praised, petted, and encouraged. Of course he'd be introduced at court, presented to the king, and who knows . . .

Abruptly Andre reined in his horse. Ahead of him the road branched, both paths leading south, neither seeming the main road. Staring down both he saw nothing that could help him decide which to take (here was still another of his strange oversights: he should have provided himself with a map of the area, either printed or a sketch by Smith, at least of the route he'd be taking). Nearby stood a house and Andre spotted a boy in the front yard (it was twelve-year-old Jesse Thorne). Unconcernedly walking his horse over he asked the boy which was the road to Tarrytown. As the boy answered, the front door of the house opened and a man came out. Andre asked him the same question, received an answer, said thank you, and touched his spurs to the horse's flanks . . .

In the attack on West Point, he thought with satisfaction, he

John Paulding, intrepid leader of Andre's captors. Shown here a bit later in life.

would have command of one of the three main assault forces, that to be directed at Fort Putnam. He'd gotten that promise from General Clinton personally. It would, of course, be vital to have it said, have it on his record, that besides masterminding the plot he'd actually led troops in combat. A few shots would be fired, and no doubt there'd be some bayonet work, but it wouldn't be much of a fight. Not with old Fort Putnam's walls weakened at strategic spots and undermanned, some of the bigger guns quietly spiked, and only a company or two of raw troops to face.

If all went well the day of the attack, he'd be allowed to have a part in the second major target, the capture of Washington himself. If possible the rebel Chief was to be taken alive. But if there were the slightest chance of failure in that, then every effort would be made to kill him, on the field of battle or elsewhere. For this he'd coordinated every detail with Arnold: At the moment Washington was at Hartford conferring with the French and in two days he was scheduled to start back to his headquarters at Tappan, reaching West Point by the 25th . . .

A well at the side of a house caught Andre's eye and he realized how dry his mouth felt, how thirsty he was. An hour had passed since he'd left Smith. He had about another hour to go. He'd stop for a cooling drink, then cover the remaining miles at a fast canter.

When he reached the well he found a little girl already there, drawing water (it was Sally Hammond, age twelve). Could he have a drink? he asked, smiling. The girl dipped a cup into the bucket and handed it up to him. He drank it slowly, gratefully, then handed the cup back. Putting his hand in his pocket he found a sixpence and gave it to the girl, saying thank you very much, little Miss. Smiling, he turned and rode off.

After cantering for a mile or two, he let the horse out at a full gallop, and the countryside began to fly past. A growing excitement gripped him, a brimming exuberance at the thought that his epic journey was near its end. Just ahead, he saw, the road led onto a small wooden bridge spanning a narrow creek. Slowing the horse to a walk, he crossed the bridge, then again spurred up.

Halt!

A man holding a musket had materialized at the side of the road. In his surprise, suddenly confused, Andre pulled back slightly on the reins but allowed the horse to walk rapidly nearer the man.

Halt! The musket was leveled, its barrel pointing straight at Andre's chest. He reined the horse to a shuffling, snorting stop as two other men slipped from behind trees and took a place in the road, muskets at the ready.

The first man, John Paulding, walked nearer, inspecting horse and rider: expensive boots, of a military type . . . good clothes . . . quality saddle and bridle . . . expensive horse with a brand on the shoulder, U.S.A.

"You're in a hurry," said Paulding. "Where you bound?"

Staring down at the man, Andre made an effort to slow his racing mind and gather his abruptly scattered thoughts. But only one fact made an impression, the green uniform jacket worn by the man.

"I see you belong to our party!" Andre blurted.

Quietly Paulding responded, "What party is that?"

"Why the lower party, of course," quickly replied Andre using the term that both sides employed to mean the British in New York City ("the upper party" was used for the Americans).

"Yes, we do," Paulding replied easily, his manner relaxed.

"Thank God!" Andre rushed on unable to stop himself. "I'm a British officer. I've been upcountry on important business for General Clinton. Please don't delay me."

Deliberately Paulding kept quiet, staring at the rider, waiting to see what else he might say.

"Here, I'll show you," said Andre reaching into his pocket. "It's all I have at the moment." He displayed an ornate gold watch of a type few besides British officers carried.

"Get down," ordered Paulding.

"I must warn you," said Andre, suddenly tense, "You're interfering with General Clinton's business, *Crown* business—"

"Get down!" repeated Paulding, adding, "we're not of the lower party. We're Americans. What's your name?"

For a moment visibly shaken, with an effort Andre recovered. "Lord!" he laughed nervously as he dismounted, "these days I have to try anything to get by! The truth is I'm not a British officer. I said that because I thought *you* were British. That Hessian jacket you're wearing . . . I was just being careful . . . you understand. My name is

Anderson. I'm American. On an important errand for General Arnold at West Point. Here, I have a pass from him."

From another pocket he took out the pass and held it toward Paulding, who accepted it, keeping his musket leveled.

Quickly scanning the few words, Paulding appeared to be impressed. "Please don't be offended," he said politely. "We mean no harm. But there are bad people all around here, Tories and traitors. We have to be careful."

Andre smiled. "Of course." He turned back to his horse to remount, putting his foot in a stirrup and reaching to draw himself up.

"Not yet, Mr. Anderson," said Paulding.

"What?"

"Come with us, in here among these trees."

Something hollow in the man's manner had disturbed Paulding's instincts, the lame way he "seemed to make a kind of laugh" of his first statement about being a British officer. To Paulding's ears the denial rang false, where his original claim about being British had sounded quite sincere.

"Listen you men," rasped Andre, his voice taking on an edge of authority as he glanced sternly at each of the three. "General Arnold has sent me to meet with an American agent in Dobbs Ferry. You are headed for serious trouble if you don't let me continue on *now!*"

Paulding nodded to his companions, and Van Wart and Williams each took hold of an arm and led Andre deep into the clump of woods.

"Just a little search, Mr. Anderson," explained Paulding, "just to be sure. Please turn out your pockets."

In the next few minutes the three went through Andre's pockets, the linings of his overcoat and jacket, felt carefully his shirt and vest as he took them off. "Now the boots and britches," directed Paulding.

"You're wasting your time!" said Andre angrily. "You're wasting *my* time! When General—"

"The boots."

Sitting down on a rock, Andre lifted his left boot, which was pulled off by Williams. Van Wart removed the right one. Each shoved a hand into a boot, said "Nothing," and handed the boot back to Andre, who bent to put them on.

"Now the stockings," directed Paulding.

Andre made no move toward his feet, only sat still staring at the ground. Van Wart reached over and pulled down the knee-length hose on the right leg. "Something in this one," he said, holding up a firm oblong shape in the sole.

Paulding took the stocking and pulled from it a thin sheaf of folded papers. "Try the other one," he said, and Van Wart quickly stripped it off. "More papers."

Together there were six sheets covered with writing in ink. Paulding went quickly over each sheet, noting especially the repeated signature of the West Point commander. From his pocket he took Arnold's pass and compared the signatures. They were nearly identical.

"These papers," he said to the other two, "are all about West Point, how many men, how many guns and where. One's about a meeting of our generals with Washington."

He turned to Andre. "Where'd you get them?"

"From a man I met at Pine's Bridge. I didn't know him. I'm to deliver them to an agent at Dobbs Ferry."

"This pass from Arnold. It's a forgery, isn't it?"

"No."

Paulding turned to his two companions. "This man's a spy! At least I think he is." Williams and Van Wart nodded their agreement.

"Get dressed," Paulding ordered, then added, "We'll take him to the dragoons at North Castle. Let them figure it out."

Sighing heavily and shaking his head, Andre said, "Gentlemen, gentlemen, I am certainly *not* a spy. I'm to deliver these papers and bring back some vital intelligence for General Arnold, as I've already—"

"Get dressed," repeated Paulding.

As Andre pulled on his ruffled shirt he turned to Paulding and in a soft, confiding tone said, "I can't explain all this to you. It's secret. But if you'll just let me ride off you'll be doing a great service for your country, and when I reach where I'm going I'll have a reward, a large reward, sent to any address you name. Here, take this gold watch, too."

Williams laughed. Curious as to why Anderson was so quick to offer a reward when he had a pass and when he claimed to be on secret business for an American general, he probed: "Will you give us your horse and saddle too? How big a reward? A hundred guineas?"

"Yes, yes, a hundred guineas. Sent anywhere you like. But the horse I'll need to get where I'm going. I'll leave it for you at Dobb's Ferry. I promise solemnly."

"Tie his arms behind his back," said Paulding to Williams.

"All right! All right!" said Andre, his tone now anxious, "Make it any sum, anything reasonable. Say a *thousand* guineas."

All three men looked at Andre's darkening face. A hundred guineas was almost as much as a working man could earn in a year. A thousand guineas in a lump was almost beyond thinking about.

"I'll write a note," explained Andre. "One of you take it into the city to a certain party and he'll pay you the money on the spot. When the money gets here, you let me go."

"In the city? You mean he's British? But you just said that you're American."

"I'm not allowed to explain any further," shot back Andre. "A thousand guineas! I'll give you an address—"

"Sure," laughed Van Wart, "then his friends would follow us back here and we'd all be done for!"

"A thousand guineas! Just send one man in and keep me here with you . . . all right make it *five* thousand . . ."

"Not for ten thousand," said Paulding quietly. "Put him on his horse. Make sure those ropes are tight."

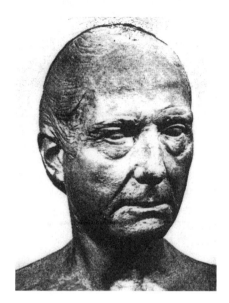

No reliable portraits have survived of the
other two militiamen who helped capture
Andre, David Williams (below), and
Isaac Van Wart. These life masks were
made when each was in old age.

Van Wart checked the ropes, then helped Andre climb up on his
horse. Paulding, his musket cradled across his arm, led the way, followed by Van Wart who had a tight hold on the reins, Williams
trudging along behind the horse. Glancing back at the prisoner, Van

Wart noticed that he'd begun to sweat, "big drops" decking his fore-head and coursing down his cheeks. "You never saw such an altera-tion in any man's face," testified Van Wart a few days later. "Only a few moments before, he was uncommonly gay in his looks, but after we made him a prisoner you could read in his face that he thought it was all over with him."

After covering a slow two miles along the dusty road in silence, the curious Williams decided he'd see if he could get the prisoner to open up a little. Would Mr. Anderson make a break for freedom, he asked teasingly, if he had the chance?

Andre glanced down disdainfully at his questioner and mumbled that he certainly would. For a moment he was silent, then in a stran-gled voice he added, "I wish to God you had blown my brains out when you stopped me!"

BUT THAT'S NOT THE WAY Andre told it.

During the ten days of his captivity, the picture of his capture offered by Andre—spun out with a disarmingly casual air—was rad-ically different. The three captors he portrayed as no better than avaricious thieves, ignorant highwaymen prowling the roads in order to rob unfortunate passersby. Some of his hearers, ready to believe anything said by, as they felt, so unfortunate and honorable a young officer, wrote down what he told them or relayed the details to others who wrote them down. Ever since, working their way into the fabric of the Andre story, they have colored and distorted the reality of that brief but momentous event.

It was by means of a clever pencil sketch that Andre made his first overt move against the three, "a ludicrous sketch of himself and his rustic escort" drawn on the evening of his arrest. To susceptible American officers he showed the little drawing, at the same time remarking that it would "give you an idea of the style in which I have had the honor to be conducted to my present abode." The sketch has not survived but it evidently pictured his three captors as little more than clowns and bumpkins.

Lieutenant Joshua King, in charge of the American post at South Salem and one of Andre's first jailers, was among those who saw the comic sketch. He records what Andre told him about the reaction of Paulding and his comrades when he showed them Arnold's pass:

> . . . damn Arnold's pass, says they. You said you was a British officer, and no money? says they. Let's search him. They did so but found none. Says one, he has got money in his boots, let's have them off and see. They took off his boots and there they found his papers but no money. They examined his saddle but found none. He said he saw they had such a thirst for money, he could put them in a way of getting it . . . Name your sum. The sum was agreed upon and . . . they held a consultation a considerable time and finally told them if he wrote [to his New York friends] a party would be sent out to take them . . .

Days later Andre was still talking about his captors, still picturing them as low creatures more interested in robbery than in protecting their country. To Captain Sam Bowman he explained that upon his claiming to be a British officer, "they seized him, robbed him of the few guineas he had with him, and the two watches which he then wore, one of gold and the other of silver." Offered a large bribe to let him go, "they hesitated," thinking it over, and declined only out of fear that they'd be caught.

Inevitably, Andre's version of the story had its most profound effect on Major Tallmadge. In view of his admitted reaction to the prisoner (never had his affections been "so fully absorbed by any man") that's not surprising, and Andre was not slow to spot the opening. As Tallmadge wrote at the time, Andre "unbosomed his heart to me . . . & indeed let me know almost every motive of his actions since coming out on his late mission."

Never did Tallmadge think to doubt any detail of Andre's self-serving story, nor did he hesitate to tell others what he'd heard from the lips of the condemned man. The three captors, he'd explain, brought their prisoner in to the American dragoon post at North Castle, "only because they thought they would get more for his surrender than for his release." He fully believed, he said, in Andre's assertions that "their object was to rob him, and that they would have let him go if he could have satisfied their demands. They took off his boots in quest of plunder, not to detect treason." The three he described as members of that slippery class of freebooters which regularly passed "between both armies, as often in one camp as the other; and whom he himself should probably have apprehended, as was always his custom, had he fallen on them."

Tallmadge's readiness to take the word of a spy from the enemy arose from more than the obvious fellow-feeling between them, from more than the fact that he was almost a mirror-image of the accomplished Englishman. It was the only way he could lift a peculiar mental burden that for many years weighed him down, the knowledge that he himself was in large part responsible for the death of the man he so greatly admired.

If it had not been for some fast thinking by Tallmadge on the evening Andre was brought in, against all expectation the prisoner would have gotten away. The plot to betray West Point would still have been defeated, but Andre would not have died.

VII

THE DAYS BEFORE — EXPOSURE

If every man is entitled to make one horrendous mistake in his life, Lieutenant Colonel John Jameson, aged twenty-eight, made his on the evening of September 23, 1780.

In temporary command of the North Castle post of the Continental Dragoons, he was on duty when the three militiamen came in with their prisoner, the supposed Mr. John Anderson. Questioning the captive about the pass he carried and the incriminating papers led nowhere, since Anderson merely repeated his story about getting them from an unknown man at Pine's Bridge in order to deliver them to another unknown man at Dobbs Ferry, all on orders from the West Point commander. Beyond that he professed to know nothing and, further, to be bound by the need for secrecy.

Colonel Jameson, ordinarily quite an able officer, resolved the situation in exactly the wrong way. He sent Anderson, still under guard as a prisoner, to none other than General Benedict Arnold in his headquarters at West Point. The six sheets of paper, however, he held back, sending them by courier to General Washington, who he knew was just then on his way back to Tappan from the Hartford conference. The courier would intercept Washington's party at Danbury, Connecticut, a forty-mile ride to the northwest, about the same

distance as from North Castle to West Point in the opposite direction.

It was the hedging decision of a cautious man, sending Anderson
without the papers back to Arnold. Not for a single moment did
Jameson question Arnold's role, never felt the slightest distrust of the
great American combat general. The pass could have been forged,
he reasoned, the papers stolen. Or the whole complicated situation
might be a clever attempt to discredit Arnold, to sow suspicion and
disrupt the good order of the American military. In that frame of
mind the obvious thing to do was to promptly inform the man at
the command center, General Arnold. But the papers, if genuine,
were too valuable to put in danger of being intercepted by the British
on the way, or to risk with anyone but the chief. That conclusion—
sending the papers one way and Andre another—wasn't really the
obvious one. On Jameson's reasoning both should have gone to Arnold. Whatever caused him to make his split decision, it saved him
and his country from total disaster.

Telling a subordinate, Lieutenant Solomon Allen, to ready a de-
tachment of a half-dozen troopers, Jameson sat down and to Arnold
penned a hasty note:

> I have sent Lt. Allen with a certain John Anderson taken going
> into New York. He had a pass signed with your name. He had
> a parcel of papers taken from under his stockings, which I think
> of a very dangerous Tendency.
>
> The Papers I have sent to General Washington. They con-
> tain the number of men at West Point and its dependencies,
> the number of cannon etc., the different pieces of Ground that
> command each fort, and what distance they are from the dif-
> ferent Forts; the situation of each Fort, and which may be set
> on fire with bombs and carcasses, and which are out of repair;
> the speech of General Washington to the Council of War held
> the sixth of this month; the situation of our armies in general,
> etc, etc.

By about seven that night, Lieutenant Allen's party with the securely bound Andre was on its way. At a normal pace—of course slowed by darkness—it would reach Arnold's headquarters in something over five hours. The courier to Washington also left at about seven, so the Chief should have the papers in his hands about midnight.

It was Ben Tallmadge, also stationed at North Castle but absent on another assignment when Andre was brought in, who saved the day, at least partially.

Returning to the post about an hour after Allen's departure, he was told by Jameson of the mysterious Mr. Anderson, the incriminating papers, and Arnold's pass. On the instant, Tallmadge saw the whole ugly plot. Without hesitation or misgiving he concluded that General Benedict Arnold had become a traitor and was conspiring with this unknown John Anderson to in some fashion betray the Revolution, probably by the fall of West Point. It was not just a wild guess, for in addition to being a dragoon officer, Tallmadge had frequently undertaken intelligence assignments for Washington, had often dealt with American spies in New York City, acting as their contact and control. No twist in the matters of allegiance and motivation, in the venal nature of many men adjudged to be great patriots, could surprise him. But he also had one other fact to help him to his startling conclusion.

This was not the first time he'd come across the name of John Anderson in connection with that of Arnold. A couple of weeks before, he'd received a letter from Arnold saying if a merchant from New York City named Anderson showed up at the North Castle post he was to be promptly sent on to West Point (this was one of the several prior attempts to set up a clandestine meeting with Andre, before the attempt succeeded at Long Clove Mountain).

No Anderson from New York had presented himself at North Castle, or at any other American post, asking for admission. But here indeed was a Mr. John Anderson, not arriving *from* New York, but caught going the other way, *to* New York, in something of a hurry, carrying vital secret information, and displaying a pass signed by Arnold.

Appalled at what Colonel Jameson had done in sending Anderson to West Point, Tallmadge blurted that Arnold was a traitor, and Jameson must immediately dispatch a fast rider to catch up to Allen and have him bring Anderson back. If he didn't, Arnold and Anderson would both escape, leaving who could tell what destruction in their wake.

Jameson refused. He couldn't at all grasp the idea of the great Arnold committing treason (not unlike many in the American service at the time). Behind his refusal, however, Jameson had another, more personal reason, also in a degree understandable: if Arnold should prove to be innocent, anyone who'd even suspected him of treason would be of no further use to the army. A Virginian, a combat-tested soldier already once wounded, Jameson was a fervent patriot who didn't want to risk losing his place in the Revolution.

When Tallmadge years later wrote about this incident, he did so with a curious hesitancy, keeping back, as he admits, some vital information. On reaching Jameson's headquarters that evening, he says, and hearing about Anderson,

> . . . I was very much surprised to find that he had been sent by Lt. Col. Jameson to Arnold's headquarters at West Point, accompanied by a letter of information respecting his capture. At the same time he dispatched an express with the papers found on John Anderson, to meet Gen. Washington, then on his way to West Point.
>
> I did not fail to state the glaring inconsistency of this conduct to Lt. Col. Jameson, in a private and most friendly manner.
>
> He appeared greatly agitated when I suggested to him a measure which I wished to adopt, offering to take the whole responsibility upon myself, and which he deemed too perilous to permit. I will not further disclose.

The capture of Andre became one of the most often depicted incidents of the Revolution, being shown in dozens of versions throughout the nineteenth century, all more or less correct. Here are shown three of them.

I finally obtained his reluctant consent to have the prisoner brought back to our headquarters. When the order was about to be dispatched to the officer to bring the prisoner back, strange as it may seem, Lt. Col. Jameson *would persist* in his purpose of letting his letter go on to Gen. Arnold. The letter did go on, and the prisoner returned before the next morning.

His determination not to "further disclose" some of the more intimate details of the incident was also mentioned in a letter he wrote a friend who had asked about it:

I have had many doubts and conflicts in my own mind, both before and since we conversed on this subject in Washington, as to the propriety & even duty of making a full Exhibition of all the incidents relating to the capture, execution, & detention of Major Andre; together with the propositions which were made to secure Gen. Arnold, and the course which was finally pursued, in consequence of which the Traitor finally escaped, even as narrowly as he did . . .

No good would be served, he adds, by telling the full story of his clash with Jameson that fateful night over the disposition of Andre, or "the proposals which were made for the detention of Gen. Arnold . . . In addition to all, I should be considered the Hero of my own Tale, without a living witness to corroborate the story." By the time of the letter Jameson was dead, and disclosure would "wound most deeply the feelings of the friends of the deceased."

What Tallmadge was hiding, of course, can be extracted from the known situation, coupled with the little he does allow himself to say. The "measure which I wished to adopt," taking full responsibility for it, and the proposal "made to secure Gen. Arnold," can mean only one thing: Tallmadge pleaded for authority to lead the full troop of dragoons, several hundred men, in a midnight dash for West Point, overtaking Andre on the way, invading Arnold's headquarters, placing the commander under peremptory arrest, and awaiting the arrival of Washington. The full troop would be needed because at that moment no one could be sure how far the despicable plot extended, how many others in positions of authority Arnold might have infected with the germ of treason. A pitched battle at West Point, Tallmadge evidently feared, not without reason, might be necessary to wrest control of the fortifications from American traitors even then readying it for surrender.

Equally clear is the fact that Jameson was stunned by the proposal. Because of "scrupulosity or weakness," he flatly refused his permission for such a daring, reckless, unheard-of action—with the result that a fierce argument ensued between the two officers. At last Jameson backed down a little, reluctantly agreeing to a compromise: he would recall Anderson but to be on the safe side would inform Arnold about what he'd done, though veiling his true reason. Again taking his pen he wrote a quick note to Lieutenant Allen:

Sir,

For some circumstances I have just heard, I have reason to fear that a party of the enemy are above; and as I would not have Anderson retaken or get away, I desire that you would proceed to lower Salem with him & deliver him to Captain Hoogland. You will leave the guard with Captain Hoogland also, except one man, whom you may take along. You may proceed on to West Point and deliver the letter to General Arnold. You may also show him this, that he may know the reason why the Prisoner is not sent on. You will please to return as soon as you can do your business.

The courier who carried that letter to Lieutenant Allen was never identified, which is a pity. His wild ride in pursuit of Allen and his party along darkened roads and through sleeping villages and open country must have been an epic one, in its own way as deserving of verse as that of Paul Revere or Sheridan's ride at Winchester. Allen had a headstart of some two hours and had to be caught before he reached Arnold's headquarters (a private house on the Hudson's eastern shore, opposite and a little below the main installations at West Point).

The route was a more or less standard one, so there was no problem about which roads to take. Also, Allen's party had proceeded at the usual pace, a mixture of canter and walk, making a steady speed of some ten miles an hour. When the courier with the letter leaped to his saddle he knew that a full gallop would carry him at a speed almost twice that of Allen's party, which by then would have crossed the Croton River at Pine's Bridge. As he raced away from dragoon headquarters he calculated that he'd catch up to his quarry somewhere this side of Peekskill.

An hour and a half of hard riding, mostly at a breakneck pace but now and then slowed down to give the horse some relief, brought the courier to within sight of Peekskill's outskirts—with no party of horse anywhere to be seen. Through the town he dashed, scattering dogs and chickens and bringing startled glances and hard looks from men and women along the streets. It was just past the north edge of town, near old St. Peter's Church, that he spotted them, the whole party of eight moving along at an easy canter.

As the surprised Lieutenant Allen turned to look at the horse that galloped up beside him he saw an animal "bloody with spurring, and fiery-red with haste."

SOUTH SALEM (CALLED "LOWER SALEM" by Jameson in his note to Lieutenant Allen) was dragoon headquarters. Located well to the north and east of North Castle, it was a more secure facility and was situated much further away from the British lines. Early on the morning of September 24, Lieutenant Allen's party and their prisoner swept noisily into the compound at South Salem to be received by the duty officer, Lieutenant Joshua King.

For Andre it had been a long and harrowing twenty-four hours, most of them spent in the saddle, and the experience was beginning to tell on him physically and emotionally. "He looked somewhat like a reduced gentleman," recalled Lieutenant King. "His small-clothes were nankeen, with handsome white-topped boots . . . his coat purple with gold lace, worn somewhat threadbare, with a small, brimmed tarnished beaver on his head. He wore his hair in a queue, with a long black beard,* and his clothes somewhat dirty. In this garb I took charge of him."

Immediately placed in a room under lock and key, Andre had two requests, that his shirt and underclothes be washed, and that he be allowed pen and paper. He wished, he said, to write directly to General Washington, explaining his situation. Both requests were granted, and King also offered him the services of a barber. Gratefully Andre accepted, and as he was being shaved, King stayed close at hand: "When the ribbon was taken from his hair I observed it full of powder; this circumstance with others that occurred, induced me to believe I had no ordinary person in charge."

Within the hour, King and everyone else would know, to their shock, precisely who it was they had in charge. This included Major Tallmadge, who'd hastened up from North Castle that afternoon to interrogate the prisoner. "As soon as I saw Anderson," he wrote, "and especially after I saw him walk (as he did almost constantly) across the floor, I became impressed with the belief that he had been bred to arms . . . I was constantly in the room with him, and he soon became very conversable and extremely interesting."

Tired and anxious as he was, Andre knew when it was time to make an impression. Promptly he'd taken the measure of his inquisitor, and by dint of being "very conversable," in that elegant way of his, let Tallmadge and no doubt the other officers present see how

---

*Andre didn't wear a beard, but he hadn't shaved in at least three days, and his hair was coal-black.

"extremely interesting" the mysterious intruder could be. When the letter Andre wrote to Washington was finished—the one read out at the trial, in which he protests against being called a spy, revealing his true identity—Tallmadge was even more impressed, though unpleasantly:

> When I received and read the letter (for he handed it to me as soon as he had written it) my agitation was extreme, and my emotions almost indescribable. If the letter of information had not gone to General Arnold, I should not have hesitated for a moment in my purpose, but I knew it must reach him before I could possibly get to West Point.

That phrase, "my purpose," of course refers to his original design to descend on West Point and arrest Benedict Arnold. With all his suspicions seemingly confirmed, in a moment of excruciating regret, he wishes that he'd ignored Jameson's prohibition and gone riding off, even if by himself alone. Now it was too late. Shortly before Tallmadge's arrival at South Salem, Lieutenant Allen after depositing his prisoner and getting a little rest had ridden away as ordered, carrying to the arch-traitor both of Jameson's tell-tale notes.

His letter to Washington finished and awaiting some means to deliver it, Andre passed the time talking with different officers at the post, most of them moved by curiosity. One of these was Isaac Bronson, post physician. He and Andre got along well and before long Andre was telling Bronson all about his capture, in the process once again denigrating the three captors, portraying them as nothing more than freebooters:

> . . . they had ripped up the housings of his saddle and the collar of his coat and, finding no money there, were upon the point of letting him go when one of the party said, "Damn him, he may have it in his boots!" They threw him down, drew off his

boots and discovered the papers, which induced the captors to think he might be a prize worth carrying in to the outposts. He offered them any sum they would name if they would let him go . . . Their reply was, a bird in the hand is worth two in the bush . . .

Never did Andre get over the galling thought that he and his master plot had been defeated by what he saw as a rustic set of ignorant farmers, in no way qualified to have played such a crucial part in the personal drama of a gentleman-officer.

THE LETTER ANDRE WROTE Washington from South Salem on the 24th was quite an able performance to have been produced under such pressure. But it mustn't be allowed to slip by unanalyzed, as up to now it has been. What more can the prettily balanced phrases tell about the young man himself? A great deal, as it turns out, especially in the subtle way he pulls and tugs at facts and ideas, twisting them deftly out of shape, and the aplomb with which he does it.

He opens by attempting to excuse his lying about himself to his captors and guards, pleading the ground of *necessity*: "What I have as yet said concerning myself was in the justifiable attempt to be extricated; I am too little accustomed to duplicity to have succeeded." He lied to get himself out of trouble, in other words. Then in the next breath he claims that he could *never* lie for "treacherous purposes or self-interest." Lying for any reason, he insists, would contravene "the principles that actuated me." Also, men of his "condition in life"—gentlemen such as you and I, General—didn't do such things.

He is not writing out of concern "for my safety," he assures Washington, but simply in order to guard his reputation against the charge of spying. As a gentleman he would *never* assume such "a mean character," would never act a part so far below his station. He was "betrayed" into his present fix, he swears, describing it as "the vile condition of an enemy in disguise within your posts." In plainer words, a spy.

The betrayal was accomplished, he adds, in spite of everything he could do to prevent it—"against my stipulation, my intention, and without my knowledge beforehand." The thing was out of his control, he means, pointedly omitting to say just *why* it was, or could be, out of his control, effectively clouding the truth. But of course he did what he did, what his cohorts told him to do, because it seemed the best thing to do at the time and in the circumstances, to him as well as to the others.

Then—of all things!—he was faced with the outright refusal of his confederates to get him out of the jam the easy way. This selfish action of his traitorous colleagues, he says, made him nothing less than "a prisoner." It was a quandary that any intelligent man of feeling and sense *must* appreciate ("Your Excellency may conceive my sensations on this occasion"), sympathize with, and forgive.

It was in these adverse circumstances, he explains, that "I quitted my uniform." Only a natural, understandable thing to do, wasn't it, assume a disguise? Understandable, and quite eminently *excusable*, wasn't it? How otherwise could a gentleman be expected to "concert his escape," and so save his reputation? Being an actual spy, a spy *de facto*, didn't really count. What mattered, what tipped the balance, was his own personal *reluctance* to do what he did, his assumed purity of heart. The great potential danger he posed to the American cause was a mere tangent, which no true gentleman would deign to notice, much less dwell on.

Adopting the tone that he did, Andre at last inevitably fell into actual impertinence. A lowly major, a youthful captive, he addresses the Commander-in-Chief as if they are equals, or even as if Andre were the social superior of the two. "The request I have to make of your Excellency, and I am conscious that I address myself well, is that in any rigor . . ." he writes. The phrase *I am conscious that I address myself well* is a courtly, roundabout way of telling someone that you believe he is your equal in proper feeling and grasp of nuance, and you want him to *know* that you consider him your equal even though he may not be, and probably isn't.

Sadly, as Andre ended his letter he somehow lost control and completely flew the track—no doubt from misapprehending the true calibre of the man he addresses. In forthright terms he utters a plain threat to retaliate on American prisoners in British jails, depending on "the treatment I receive." Such a barefaced threat, he knew, would never work on him or on any of his superiors. Why did he think it would work with Washington? More to the point, he here utterly contradicts his opening claim that he wasn't concerned "for my safety," didn't wish to "solicit security."

Closing, he again feels he must assume a superior air while cleverly veiling it with seeming deference. "It is no less, Sir, in a confidence in the generosity of your mind, than on account of your superior station, that I have chosen to importune you with this letter." What exactly is he saying? This: if I didn't think you were a high-minded gentleman like myself I wouldn't bother writing at all even though my fate is in your hands. To be judged rightly, in other words, Andre's case needed someone who understood and adhered to the code of a gentleman above all.

In its controlled phrasing and its elaborate juggling of facts and ideas, the famous letter in reality affords a prime example of Andre's usual technique in weaving his spell on a *listening* audience, people in the flesh. Reduced to writing, as here, that technique is a good deal less impressive than it may have seemed when, framed by ingratiating smiles, it came rolling off his tongue.

BREAKFAST AT BENEDICT ARNOLD'S HEADQUARTERS was served early, about seven. On September 25 as he sat down with his officers, Arnold was full of anxiety and apprehension, though his noted facility for outward self-control kept his feelings hidden. Andre, he calculated, should have reached British headquarters in New York City by noon of the 23rd, the day after he left Haverstraw. The 24th should have seen the three ships of the assault force begin their movement upriver. No sail had yet been sighted, but at any moment some excited sentry might raise the alarm.

Washington and his party, according to the official schedule provided to commanders, had left Hartford on the return to Tappan early on the 24th. Normal speed of progress would bring them to West Point just at the proper moment for the Chief's capture, whether before or during the battle. Either way, Washington was sure to take personal command in the emergency, leaving himself open to a hand-picked raiding party.

The plan, admittedly a complicated one, was working nicely. Hundreds of the regular troops had been dispersed, scattered over the hills in wood-chopping and road-mending parties, while others had been stationed in exposed positions. The main body in the principal forts had been left without sufficient officers or specific orders. The waiting for things to get started, that was the hard part.

An aide entered and handed Arnold at the table an envelope. It had just arrived by express from South Salem, he explained. The rider was standing by to see if there was any response. In the envelope were two short notes, one from Colonel Jameson announcing the capture of Mr. Anderson, the other from Jameson to Lieutenant Allen countermanding the delivery of Anderson to West Point.*

Sitting at the table, Arnold read both notes without turning a hair. Replacing them in the envelope, for several minutes he sat talking with his officers, his manner relaxed. Then he said casually that he had some business to attend to over at the Point. Standing up, he reminded his officers that General Washington would be along before noon. He'd be back in time to greet him personally, he said, then turned and walked calmly out of the room.

---

*Lieutenant Allen's arriving at West Point the morning of the 25th rather than the evening of the 24th has never been explained. See the Notes for some discussion.

It was about ten o'clock when Washington's party came bustling and clattering into the main yard to be greeted by a contingent of waiting officers. General Arnold wasn't there at the moment, one of them apologized, but should be along any minute. Some business had called him across the river. Washington, a bit surprised at this neglect of protocol, said that he and his party hadn't stopped for breakfast, so they'd eat while they waited.

An hour later Arnold still hadn't shown up. Breakfast finished, Washington said that since one of his reasons for the visit was to inspect the forts, he'd go over to the Point rather than wait. No doubt he'd catch up to Arnold there. Accompanied by two aides he set out to tour the entire sprawling complex. He could hardly believe what he found:

> As Washington made the rounds, he encountered shocking conditions of past bad planning and of present neglect. Fort Arnold, built of dry fascines and wood, was incomplete and manifestly could be set afire by shells. The eastern wall of Fort Putnam had fallen; its chevaux de frise was broken in many places; it was commanded altogether at a distance of 500 yards by Rocky Hill, where the fortification was feeble, particularly on the side an enemy was apt to assail.
>
> Almost every part of the stronghold of the Hudson was decayed, or incomplete, or inflammable. It was tempting Providence in that year of disappointment to have West Point exposed and indefensible . . .
>
> Strangely enough very few men were visible as garrison or as masons. At each of the forts and redoubts Washington inquired for Arnold. Nobody had seen him. The commander of the post, Col. John Lamb, said that so far as he knew Arnold had not set foot there during the morning. Washington felt some irritation that an officer of Arnold's experience should have been negligent in attendance when word of the visit of the Commander-in-Chief had been sent . . .

By mid-afternoon, his inspection tour complete, Washington had returned to Arnold's headquarters, his head full of "vague misgivings." As he entered the building an aide handed him two sealed envelopes, one large and bulky, the other small and thin. They'd been delivered a little while before, the aide said, by an express rider from South Salem. Reading the various papers Washington was again severely shocked, this time receiving such a blow as he "never had sustained" before.

The larger envelope contained the six documents about the West Point defenses found on Andre, along with a letter from Jameson explaining the circumstances of the capture. The smaller envelope held the personal letter to Washington written by Andre. (The courier sent to catch Washington at Danbury had missed him and had returned to South Salem, when he was again dispatched, this time to West Point. While at South Salem the Andre letter had been added to the pouch.)

Dismayed and disbelieving ("Whom can we trust now!" he said to Hamilton), Washington still remained the self-possessed leader he'd shown himself for five harrowing years. Questioning Arnold's officers he learned about the note delivered that morning to him at breakfast and his departure from the table shortly afterward. That fact, together with Arnold's continued absence and the weakened condition of West Point, along with the six documents and Andre's letter of confession (it amounted to that), instantly brought the entire plot to his mind, clear and undeniable. He also promptly guessed Arnold's probable escape route.

Colonel Hamilton! he said urgently, take two men and ride at top speed for wherever the *Vulture* is anchored. Arnold has gone downriver and will try to board her. Stop him any way you can, but if possible bring him back unharmed. Asking no questions, Hamilton motioned to two men and all three went racing out the door.

For the remaining hours of that day and far into the night, Washington issued a stream of orders, shoring up the West Point defenses, assigning new officers in all the more critical positions (there was no time to make sure of the existing ones), and alerting and mobilizing all American forces within a hundred miles. He also ordered that Major Andre be brought to West Point, under a strong guard of at least a full troop. The British, he reasoned, might have sent out a raiding party to recover their man along the way.

Rather quickly the name of Joshua Smith came up, when reports began to filter in from the ferrymen at Stony and Verplanck's points and from Captain Boyd and Lieutenant Foote. No one on Arnold's staff had a good word for Smith, seeing him as a shadowy figure of doubtful allegiance whose link with Arnold they had always resented as at least unwise. Before dark Washington had dispatched a squad of men to track him down and by midnight he'd been located at the home of a relative in Fishkill, some eighteen miles north of West Point. As Smith recalled the arrest, the door of the room in which he and his wife lay asleep "was forced open with great violence, and instantly the chamber was filled with soldiers, who approached the bed with fixed bayonets."

Back at headquarters he was taken to a room where he found Washington with several officers waiting. As Smith entered, at the room's center towered the Chief, his face scowling ("looked sternly and with much indignation at me"). Smith stood charged with "the blackest treachery against the citizens of the United States," he was scathingly informed, in which he was liable to summary execution. He knew nothing of any treachery! replied the quavering Smith. The traitor Arnold had fled, he was told, but Andre the British spy ("whom *you* piloted through our lines!") was in American hands. Unless Smith made a prompt and full confession naming all accomplices, growled Washington pointing out a window, "I'll suspend you *both* on yonder tree!" Take him away, he ended.

Soon after dark Hamilton returned from his dash down to the *Vulture*. He'd been much too late, he reported, for Andre's longboat had been sighted by many along the way and had approached the

British sloop under a flag of truce. In fact at Verplanck's Point two letters from the ship to Washington, sent ashore earlier, awaited him. One was from Arnold, the other from Beverly Robinson. Arnold's turned out to be a piece of pure effrontery, claiming "love to my country" as his motive for the treason—"however it may appear inconsistent to the world"—and begging indulgence for his wife, who he says knew nothing of his intentions (left behind at headquarters by her husband's precipitate departure, she had indulged in some brief hysterics and supposedly knew nothing of the plot. On that one the jury is still out).

The Robinson note, in its way, was even more brazen, for it calmly advanced a claim which could never be taken seriously:

> Major Andre cannot be detained by you without the greatest violation of flags, and contrary to the custom and usage of all nations; and as I imagine you will see this matter in the same point of view that I do, I must desire you will order him to be set at liberty and allowed to return immediately. Every step Major Andre took was by the advice and direction of General Arnold, and even that of taking a feigned name, and of course not liable to censure for it.

It was of course no more than a bold attempt to intimidate (based on Arnold's lying, self-defensive claim made aboard ship that Andre had landed under a flag of truce). No one on the British side needed to be told that truce flags did not legitimize clandestine activity. Still, it was a good try: who knew whether the untested leaders of the neophyte nation might not be spooked by a simple accusation of *gaucherie?*

LOCKED IN A WINDOWLESS ROOM at dragoon headquarters in South Salem, Andre couldn't see the rain but he could hear it, a heavy downpour now and then slackening off only to come roaring up

Self-sketch made by Andre the evening before his execution, when he still expected to be reprieved. His captors declared it a very good likeness.

again. When Lieutenant King entered to tell him that he was to be transferred immediately to West Point, he sighed at the thought of still more weary hours in the saddle, another night ride, this one an exceedingly wet one.

Still, he told himself, he'd be meeting Washington all the sooner, and that was important, giving him a chance to plead his case in person. There was no reason why the American Chief should not react as favorably to him personally as had all the other American officer's he'd met at the North Castle and South Salem posts. Some things were so much more effective when spoken, the voice warmly confiding, than when written down, such as the comments in his letter to Washington about his having entire "confidence in the generosity of your mind," and that having "avowed myself a British officer I have nothing to reveal but what relates to myself, which is true on the honor of an officer and a gentleman," or that he be "branded with nothing dishonorable." Those sincere little comments he was prepared to repeat and expand, so soon as he was at West Point and had the general's ear.

The troop, with Andre bound and mounted near the column's middle, set off from South Salem before midnight. "The rain fell in torrents," wrote Dr. Bronson afterwards, "and it was the darkest and most miserable night I have ever known. On taking leave he expressed a deep sense of the obligation he was under" to the American for all their kind attentions (for their "delicate and courteous deportment" is the way Andre phrased it). Saying goodbye, Dr. Bronson assured the prisoner that "whatever might be his future destiny, he would never meet them hereafter as enemies."

It was dawn as the soaked troop arrived at headquarters in West Point. Andre was taken to a separate room in the building and locked in with a guard. All day he waited to be called for questioning by Washington, unaware that Smith was a captive in another room not far from him. As each hour passed, and as one guard was replaced by another in the room, his expectation of a summons by Washington mounted. At last in the early evening the door opened and an officer appeared.

The prisoner, he announced, would be taken across the river and held for a night or two in a secure jail at Fort Putnam. He would then be sent down to the main army camp at Tappan. There he would face a formal court of inquiry to decide the question he raised in his letter to the Commander-in-Chief, whether he was to be deemed a soldier or a spy.

There would be no meeting with Washington.

PART THREE

VIII

FAREWELL PERFORMANCE

His eyelids flickered up at the first faint touch of daylight. With open eyes fixed on the ceiling he lay on the bed, dimly aware of the officer sitting in a chair in the far corner of the room. He'd dozed off but only for a minute or two.

The whole interminable night had passed like that, briefly dozing and suddenly waking to lie there with his mind either racing wildly or slowed to dull immobility. It was just after dawn, he saw, which meant that some seven hours of life were left to him and then it would be all over. By noontime he would be dead.

The negotiations between the generals to arrange his exchange had failed. He'd been told of the failure the previous evening by Colonel Laurence, who also informed him that his execution would take place at noon the next day, Monday, October 2.

He'd known all along that death was a possibility of course. When the decision of the court reached him the first time, on the evening of the 30th, it had hit him with devastating impact and for a few awful moments he'd actually felt his skin shudder and crawl, his arms and legs tremble. The reaffirmation of the sentence on the previous evening had left him numb but steady. His first thought, in fact, was for the manner of execution, the way it would be done. Death for spies, as he knew, by the custom of all nations was at the end of a rope (within his own experience was the case of the American spy, Nathan Hale, given no trial but summarily hung by order of General Clinton's predecessor, General Howe, in New York City). It was a form of final judgment abhorred by any true gentleman, particularly a military gentleman. For an officer, the firing squad was the only approved method of execution, and Andre hadn't hesitated to request it for himself. The evening of the 1st he'd addressed Washington directly in a letter, even here being unable to keep from emphasizing his personal worth, his individual excellence:

Sir,

Buoy'd above the terror of death by the consciousness of a life devoted to honorable pursuits, and stained with no action that can give me remorse, I trust that the request I make to your Excellency at this serious period, and which is to soften my last moments, will not be rejected.

Sympathy towards a soldier will surely induce your Excellency and a military tribunal, to adapt the mode of my death to the feelings of a man of honor.

Let me hope, Sir, that if aught in my character impresses you with esteem towards me, if aught in my misfortune marks me as the victim of policy and not of resentment, I shall experience the operation of these feelings in your breast, by being informed that I am not to die on a gibbet . . .

From Washington had come no reply to the request, and Andre gratefully took the silence, the absence of a refusal, to mean that his dying hope would be granted. He felt even surer of it when told that, though he'd been convicted as a spy disguised in civilian clothes, he would be permitted by order of the Chief himself to go to his execution wearing his regimental uniform (the scarlet jacket had been recovered from its hiding place at the Smith house).

With that, Andre entered what can only be described as a radically altered state of mind, a strange mood of exaltation, perhaps possible only to a practiced dissembler. He would, he determined, set the rebels and the watching world such an example of sheer courage, of graceful self-control and mental command in the face of life's most harrowing moment, as would make his name and fate a by-word in military history. Andre the woefully bumbling secret agent would be forgotten. Remembered and written about in song and story would be the marvelous figure of the brave young officer who gave his life for his country, who went as a gentleman uncomplainingly to a needless and unjust death.

The remarkable performance began the moment he rose from his restless night's sleep and sat down to a leisurely breakfast, conversing pleasantly with his guards, both of them visibly nervous.

His personal servant from New York City, Peter Laune, who'd been with him for some years, was allowed to come up and attend him. As soon as breakfast was over he sat down to have Laune shave him and dress and powder his hair, rebraiding the short queue and tying it with a bit of leather ribbon in military fashion.

Pulling on his stockings he could not have helped reflecting that his single unwise act of concealing the West Point papers under his bare feet, disobeying the explicit orders he'd been given about *not* carrying any papers, had been his downfall. If no incriminating documents had been found . . .

Britches and polished boots followed, then the ruffled shirt, freshly laundered, the vest and neckcloth, and the scarlet, gold-trimmed jacket (if only he'd never taken it *off*!). Seeing his slender, handsome young master so splendidly attired again, realizing that in a very few hours he would be removing the colorful jacket from a dead body (he was to take it back to New York for return to Andre's family), Laune could not hold back the tears.

Andre cast an annoyed look at his distressed servant. "Leave me," he ordered brusquely, "until you can show yourself more manly!" The

Andre's prison-room at the Mabie Tavern, showing him on the morning of his execution. At the left, Colonel Scammell reads Washington's order imposing the death penalty.

unduly harsh tone was noticed in surprise by the two guards in the room—Captains John Hughes and Samuel Bowman—and they silently wondered at it. Out the door hastened the contrite Laune, never realizing that, with his sentimental display, he'd simply gotten in the way of his master's farewell performance. In the script now running through Andre's deftly calculating mind there was no place for tears. Any hint of sadness, melancholy, or regret would mar the effect.

By ten o'clock or a little later he was ready (that was important to him, being ready well before he was called). Gentlemen, he said to Hughes and Bowman as he took his tricorn uniform hat off a hook and laid it on the small round table at the room's center, I'm ready to proceed at any moment. Sitting down at the table he went on talking, his voice calm and even, his manner unconcerned. During the half-hour the three conversed not a word passed Andre's lips about the day's main event, only general comments and inquiries about the two guards' military careers and their families.

As they talked, there sounded the low rumble of muffled drums approaching, accompanied by the sharp peal of fifes, faintly at first, then growing louder. Outside the tavern the music ceased and commands were called out to the lines of troops. Andre got up and went to the window to look out. It's my escort, he said, adding that quite a large crowd of civilians had already congregated along both sides of the street. We shall not be without a sufficient audience, he said, smiling.

The door opened to admit Colonel Alexander Scammell, the army's Adjutant-General. It's time, Major, he announced in a low voice. Are you ready?

Certainly, Colonel, replied Andre as he stood, picked up his hat, and fixed it carefully on his head.

Hughes and Bowman came up to stand on either side of the prisoner. Scammell read out the brief execution order, then turned and exited, followed by the other three. When they stood side by side on the porch, Andre abruptly linked his arms with those of his two guards and deliberately hurried them forward, carrying them speedily down the steps and into line. The satisfied little smile on Andre's face struck Colonel Scammell as being a bit bizarre.

Behind, ranks of soldiers four abreast filled the entire length of the street. Just in front was a flatbed wagon on which lay, lengthwise, a coffin painted black. Ahead of the wagon walked the fife-and-drum army band, with more ranks of four-abreast troops leading the procession. In front as officer of the day rode General John Glover with four aides, two colonels, and two majors.

"I am much surprised to find your troops under so good discipline," offered Andre to Scammell, "and your music is excellent."

It was precisely the wrong note to sound, the only misstep of the day, much too lofty and superior to pass as a sincere compliment. In striving for effect, Andre had overreached himself. If Scammell and the others caught the condescension, the false ring of the remark, they never said. Spoken in the emotion of the moment perhaps it did make Andre seem forgiving and above it all.

Asked if he preferred to ride in the wagon, Andre said no, he didn't at all mind walking. Scammell lifted his hand and made a signal and from the band rose the slow, mournful strains of the "Dead March." The procession began moving.

The crowds all along the street and up the hill after the turn to the left out of the village were silent, staring sober-faced at the prisoner as he passed by. Andre's expression was the opposite, showing a fixed smile, now slight as his gaze swept over the packed onlookers, now broadening and accompanied by a courtly bow as he recognized one or another of the fourteen generals who had condemned him or one of the officers who'd served as guards in his room.

Tears came to the eyes of many along the way, men as well as women, to see such bravery in one so young, such mastery of himself and his emotions. However, not everyone was taken by this aspect of the drama. "Such fortitude I never was witness of," recalled army physician John Hart, "nor ever had I such disagreeable feelings at an execution, to see a man go out of time without fear but all the time smiling."

Another eyewitness, James Thatcher, also an army physician, captured the incongruous behavior, apparently feeling some of the same sense of disproportion though expressing it less forcefully. He couldn't it seems, quite decide what to make of it. Andre, he said, walked out of the stone house,

> between two of our subaltern officers arm in arm; the eyes of the immense multitude were fixed on him who, rising superior to the fears of death, appeared as if conscious of the dignified deportment which he displayed. He betrayed no want of fortitude, but maintained a complacent smile on his countenance,

and politely bowed to several gentlemen whom he knew, which
was respectfully returned . . .

As if conscious of the impression he was making. An incisive observation indeed. Too bad Dr. Thatcher didn't explain just what it
was he saw or felt which convinced him that the graciously smiling
prisoner was aware of the impression he made.

At the hill's summit the mounted leaders swung left into a narrower road with only a house or two set well back among the trees.
Another slight rise took the procession still higher—and then Andre
caught sight of the huge crowd surrounding a large open area, all
kept back by hundreds of soldiers forming a hollow square. It was
what Andre saw looming at the center of the square that stopped
him in his tracks with a sharp intake of breath. It was a gallows.

"What's the matter?" asked Captain Bowman.

Momentarily the iron composure broke. Convulsively raising his
hand and pointing, he asked in a loud voice, "*Must* I die in this
manner? I'm reconciled to my death, but not like this! Did General
Washington receive my request to be shot?"

Major Tallmadge, in the procession some yards behind the prisoner, came up. Yes, he said, the general received your note. He decided he could not alter the accepted method without calling in
question your status as a spy. He said he regretted it very much but
concluded it was unavoidable.

Why did he not inform me of the decision?

He thought it better to spare your last hours, leave you some hope.
He went as far as he could in allowing the use of your uniform.

Pausing, Tallmadge added apologetically, Some of us, Colonel
Hamilton and others, tried to change his mind . . . he said he was
sorry but he could not do it . . .

His head lowered, Andre turned back into the line of march. "It
is a hard fate for a soldier," he mumbled.

Nearby in a line stood several of the men who'd had some part in Andre's captivity, among them Tallmadge, Lieutenant King, Hamilton, and the three captors. To Tallmadge Andre made a sign, beckoning him forward. As the American walked up, Andre grasped his hand. Goodbye, he said warmly. It has been a pleasure to know you. Remember me. Tallmadge, his eyes wet, his throat tightening, unable to offer any response, stepped back.

Repeating the action with Hamilton and King, Andre ended by waving to all and saying loudly, "It will be but a momentary pang."

The three captors he pointedly ignored.

Major, said Scammell, please get up on the wagon.

Ignoring the step placed at the wagon's tailboard, Andre grasped the edge of the tailboard and tried to vault up all at once, but he didn't make it and had to drop back down. Lifting one knee, he placed it on the wagon and carefully hoisted himself. Straightening, he stood a moment looking at the coffin. Then he stepped up atop the closed lid, placed his hands on his hips, and sauntered several times back and forth. Standing still, he removed his hat and with his head held high, let his gaze roam over the assemblage of spectators, civilian and military. The one face he was hoping to see was that of the Commander-in-Chief, the one man he very much wanted to have present. If Washington was there, Andre failed to spot him (he wasn't).

At the front of the wagon another man climbed up, his face blackened with soot (to hide his identity). Andre saw him and stepped down from the coffin, walking to the rear edge of the wagon just beneath the dangling noose. His hat he let drop on the coffin.

Do you wish to say anything, Major? called up Scammell from beside the wagon.

Looking down at Scammell, then throwing a glance at the others gathered nearby, Andre paused for what seemed to his hearers like minutes though it was merely seconds. At last he spoke, the words carrying clear and deliberate in the mild air: "Only this, gentlemen, that you all bear me witness that I meet my fate like a brave man."

It was almost another false note, more evident later when the emotions of the moment had cooled. Andre need not have invited witnesses to do what they were all quite prepared to do unasked, bear personal testimony to his marvelous command of himself, his unprecedented degree of casual bravery amounting nearly to unconcern. There was no need for him to state the obvious. Further, on hearing Andre's statement, or being told of it—his words raced through the crowd as one man told another—quite a few were struck by the sharp contrast with the last words uttered by the young American spy, Nathan Hale, four years earlier. They'd been a lot more inspiring and memorable than Andre's self-contemplating request. "I only regret that I have but one life to lose for my country," said the schoolteacher-turned-soldier just before the rope tightened.

Did he wish to have a blindfold? asked the hangman.

From his pocket Andre drew a large silk handkerchief which he twirled into a flat strip, placed over his eyes, and tied at the back of his head. Then he took off his neckcloth and opened the button of his shirt. When he felt the hangman placing the noose over his head he snapped, "Take your black hands off me!" in a low tone heard only by those nearest the wagon.

Reaching up he snatched the noose from the soot-blackened hands and drew it down over his head. The thick knot he carefully positioned under his right ear, drawing it tight.

Bind his arms too, called the watching Scammell.

Andre pulled the blind down from his eyes, reached into another pocket, and drew out another large silk handkerchief. Twirling it into a flat strip, he handed it to the hangman, then replaced the blind over his eyes. The hangman pulled both arms back and tied them at the elbows. Then he jumped down from the wagon and walked around to the front, taking hold of the reins of the two horses.

Colonel Scammell drew his sword and held it out level at arm's length. For a moment he stood still. Then down came the blade, a whip cracked, and there sounded a sudden jumble of hooves. "The wagon was very suddenly drawn from under the gallows," one soldier described the sight that followed, "which together with the length of the rope gave him a most tremendous swing back and forth; but in a few moments he hung entirely still . . . He remained hanging, I should think, from twenty to thirty minutes, and during that time the chambers of death were never stiller than the multitude by which he was surrounded."

Others present also remembered how a deep hush settled over the scene, how "all the spectators seemed to be overwhelmed . . . suffused in tears." Major Tallmadge stared through brimming eyes at the limp corpse: "When I saw him swinging under the gibbet, it seemed for a time as if I could not support it."

A grave had been dug in the field the day before not far from the gallows but had been hidden under canvas to spare the doomed man's feelings. Now the wagon was driven over to the uncovered grave, the coffin unloaded and laid on the ground beside it. The dead man was taken down, two soldiers cradling the body to prevent its falling while a third cut the rope. Dr. Hart bent over the prostrate figure and after an examination of a few moments, nodded. The two men lifted the body and carried it over to the coffin. Before laying it in they paused to remove the scarlet tunic.

The crowd had already formed itself into long lines, ready to view the corpse. The press of people, recalled one man, was "so great that it was some time before I could get an opportunity . . . I viewed the corpse more carefully than I had ever done that of any human being before. His head was very much on one side, in consequence of the manner in which the halter drew upon his neck. His face appeared to be greatly swollen, and very black, much resembling a high degree of mortification. It was indeed a shocking sight to behold."

By mid-afternoon the crowd had melted away, and the soldiers had been marched off, leaving only a burial squad. Standing at attention as the coffin was closed and lowered into the grave were Tallmadge, Hamilton, LaFayette, and a few others.

No headstone was erected, only a small pile of stones laid out to mark the location. A few days later someone planted cedar trees at either end. On the grave itself an unknown woman planted a peach tree.

DURING FORTY YEARS, as one century ended and another began, while Andre's story was repeatedly told, his praises sung in poems, plays, and novels, his grave received little attention. A strong sentiment in the Tappan neighborhood felt that any slightest honor paid to Andre or his grave constituted an insult to the memory of Washington, so little or nothing was done to mark his resting place. In 1818 a visiter to Tappan, Captain Alden Partridge, a professor at West Point, wrote in his journal that "The place is distinctly marked at a distance by two small cedars about 8 feet high, one of which has grown out of the southeast corner of the grave, and the other on the north side . . . the grave can be plainly distinguished—it has a small head and foot stone, but without any inscription, and is encompassed by a small enclosure of rough stones loosely placed upon each other" (the "stones" at head and foot were just that, small rocks). Within a year of Partridge's visit someone rolled a small boulder to the site and had an inscription cut in it: "Andre Executed Oct 2nd 1780." The neglect of the grave ended in the summer of 1821 when Andre's remains were transferred from the lonely isolation of Tappan to England's pantheon of heroes and honored dead, Westminster Abbey. There had been talk years earlier about making the transfer but a variety of circumstances interfered, then the second war with England, the War of 1812, canceled all such plans.

On the morning of August 10, 1821, a British naval vessel, the frigate *Phaeton*, sailed up the Hudson following much the same track as the *Vulture* forty years before. Opposite Dobbs Ferry, just off Sneden's Landing, it anchored and the British consul from New York City, James Buchanan, with a large party of ladies and gentlemen came ashore. A parade of carriages took them the four miles to

Tappan. Waiting to welcome them at the gravesite was a large contingent of Americans.

At the Mabie Tavern the party made a brief stop, the owner showing them the room used as a prison for Andre (actually his bedroom,
the owner not understanding that he also had the use of a sitting
room). "Excited as we were," wrote Buchanan of the visit, "it would
be difficult to describe our feelings on entering this little chamber;
it was then used as a milk and store room—otherwise unaltered from
the period of his confinement—about twelve feet by eight, with one
window looking into the garden."

Trudging up the hill the party came to the open field at the summit, Buchanan all the while wondering about the rumors he'd heard
claiming that the grave had been despoiled long before, the body
perhaps stolen. The extensive plot of ground, he saw in some surprise,
was completely under cultivation, but he soon found that an effort
had been made to spare the grave. The field itself

> . . . contained from eight to ten acres, and was cultivated; but
> around the grave the plow had not approached nearer than
> three or four yards, that space being covered with loose stone
> thrown upon and around the grave, which was indicated by
> two cedar trees about ten feet high; a small peach tree had also
> been placed at the head of the grave by the kindly feeling of
> a lady in the neighborhood . . . the day was unusually fine; a
> number of ladies and many aged matrons who witnessed his
> fall, who had mingled tears with his sufferings, attended . . .

The crowd ringing the site was kept back at a distance, and no
time was lost in setting the diggers to work. The shovels were wielded
with care so as not to penetrate the hard-packed earth too deeply or
too forcefully:

> The laborers proceeded with diligence, yet caution; surmises
> about the body having been removed were revived, and it

Memorial stone presently occupying the site of Andre's execution at Tappan, New York. It was erected by an American "in token of those better feelings which have since united" the two countries.

The Andre monument in Westminster Abbey. The bas-relief sculpture panel in the middle depicts his capture.

would be difficult to imagine any event which could convey a degree of more excitement.

As soon as the stones were cleared away and the grave found, not a tongue moved amongst the multitude—breathless anxiety was depicted in every countenance. When at length one of the men cried out that he had touched the coffin, so great was the enthusiasm at this moment that I found it necessary to call the aid of several of the ladies to form an enlarged circle so that all could see the operation; which being effected, the men proceeded with the greatest caution and the clay was removed with the hands, as we soon discovered the lid of the coffin was broken in the center.

With great care the broken lid was removed, and there to our view lay the bones of the brave Andre, in perfect order. I, amongst others, for the first time discovered that he had been a small man. This observation I made from the skeleton, which was confirmed by some then present. The roots of the small peach tree had completely surrounded the skull like a net.

After allowing all the people to pass around in regular order and view the remains as they lay, which very many did with unfeigned tears and lamentations, the bones were carefully removed and placed in the sarcophagus . . .

A contemporary newspaper report of the event explained that when the broken lid was taken off, "the skeleton of the brave Andre appeared entire, bone to bone, each in its place, without a vestige of any other part of his remains save some of his hair which appeared in small tufts, [and] the leather string which tied it."

The large, square sarcophagus (properly an ossuary) in which the bones would be transported to London had been supplied by the duke of York, uncle of the future Queen Victoria. Made to order in New York City, it was fashioned of polished mahogany, with exterior panels of crimson velvet edged with gold. The interior was lined with rich black velvet.

Curiously, Buchanan didn't know that Andre's regimental tunic had been removed before burial, but had heard rumors to that effect and very much wanted to settle the point. The bones having been removed,

> I descended into the coffin, which was not more than three feet below the surface, and with my own hands raked the dust together to ascertain whether he had been buried in his regimentals or not, as it was rumored by the assemblage that he had been stripped; for if buried in his regimentals I expected to find the buttons of his clothes which would disprove the rumor. But I did not find a single button . . .

With the ceremonies at the grave concluded, the officials stepped back into their carriages and the procession slowly wound its way down to the Hudson River. There the dead Andre was taken aboard the *Phaeton*, making the short journey from shore to ship that the living Andre might easily have made some forty years before, preserving his own life and radically altering the course of American and world history.

IX

ANDRE'S REVENGE

They had only a brief moment on the stage. They knew little of the larger forces surrounding them, and they were only doing their duty. But if it had not been for John Paulding and his two companions the story of America would have been vastly different. In halting Andre that September morning, at a stroke they did more to shape America's future, and in a degree that of the world, than all the nation's celebrated heroes and statesmen combined. Afterward, unaffected by the fame that enveloped them, all three went back to farming, living ordinary lives and raising families. Paulding lived another thirty-eight years, Van Wart another forty-eight, and Williams another fifty.

In all that time only a single incident occurred to mar the public perception of the captors' crucial role in the Revolution. That happened when the avenging hand of Andre reached across the years to lay its icy grip on the heart of Ben Tallmadge, stirring his old feeling of remorse.

At first, in the flurry of excitement over the discovery of the plot and the fate of Andre, the three were overlooked, shunted into the background. Washington, making his initial report to Congress on the Arnold affair a few days after the exposure, admitted, "I do not know the party that took Major Andre, but it is said that it consisted only of a few militia, who acted in such a manner upon the occasion as does them the highest honor, and proves them to be men of great virtue." He'll send the names along shortly, he adds.

A week later while reporting the results of Andre's trial to Congress he writes: "I now have the pleasure to communicate the names of the three persons who captured Major Andre, and who refused to release him notwithstanding the most earnest importunities and assurances of a liberal reward on his part. Their names are *John Paulding, David Williams,* and *Isaac Van Wart.*" He'd made it a point to meet and shake hands with all three at Tappan on the day of Andre's execution.

In the same letter he notes the crucial nature of the captors' service, so much so that he takes the unusual step of suggesting that a tangible reward was in order: "Their conduct merits our warmest esteem; and I beg leave to add that I think the public would do well to allow them a handsome gratuity. They have prevented in all probability our suffering one of the severest strokes that could have been meditated against us." Promptly on receiving Washington's recommendation, Congress acted, passing a resolution on November 3rd:

Whereas, Congress have received information that John Paulding, David Williams, and Isaac Van Wart, three young volunteer militia-men of the State of New York, did on the 23rd day of September last, intercept Major John Andre, Adjutant-General of the British Army, on his return from the American lines in the character of a Spy; and, notwithstanding the large bribes offered them for his release, nobly disdaining to sacrifice their country for the sake of Gold, secured and conveyed him to the Commanding officer of the district, whereby the dangerous and traitorous conspiracy of Benedict Arnold was brought to light, the insidious designs of the enemy baffled, and the United States rescued from impending danger: RE-SOLVED,

That Congress have a high sense of the virtuous and

patriotic conduct of the said John Paulding, David Williams, and Isaac Van Wart:—*In Testimony whereof*: ORDERED, that each of them receive annually out of the Public Treasury Two Hundred Dollars in specie, an equivalent in current money of these States, during life, and that the Board of war procure for each of them a silver Medal, on one side of which shall be a Shield with this inscription: *"Fidelity,"*—and on the other the following motto, *"Vincit Amor Patriae,"*—and forward them to the Commander-in-Chief, who is requested to present the same, with a copy of this Resolution, and the thanks of Congress for their Fidelity, and the eminent service they have rendered their country.

Prosecution of the war, then going none too well, occupied everyone's attention, delaying preparation of the medals and their presentation, even more so with the shifting of the main army to Yorktown in Virginia. With the fall of Yorktown to Washington in the fall of 1781, and with victory for the rebels in sight, the war began to wind down. But another year was to pass before the three men received their medals. When they did get them, it was handsomely done.

Washington and his army were again up north, again camped in the West Point area. In September 1782 the Americans were hosts to their French allies and for several weeks there was almost a festive air among the troops with full-dress uniforms being displayed at banquets, parades, and ceremonial oservances. It was during one of these events that the three captors were publically honored, receiving their medals (the first such awards ever struck by Congress) from the hands of Washington himself. That night at a banquet they sat at Washington's table, and each was presented with a sword and a brace of pistols, personal gifts from the Commander-in-Chief. To each he also offered a commission as captain in the regular army, to begin after the war. All three declined, preferring to return home.

At that point for two of the three, military life was at an end: Washington himself had warned that they'd "be hunted like partridges" by the avenging British, so to be safe they should leave active service. John Paulding, however, continued as a member of the Westchester militia and in 1783 in one of the last skirmishes of the war he was badly wounded and again taken prisoner (the wound, by bayonet or sword, may have been inflicted in anger when his identity as a captor of Andre became known). Promptly Washington was informed that Paulding was in British hands and he immediately and personally began making preparations for an exchange. But there was no need. Hostilities terminated and the Revolution came to an end. Paulding was released from his New York City prison hospital and he went happily home, to suffer for some years from his wound.

For all three the grateful state of New York also had a benefit to bestow. Each was allowed to choose a farm of up to five hundred acres anywhere in the state. Van Wart preferred to stay near his old home at Tarrytown, choosing a farm at Mount Pleasant. Williams first found one that suited him at Eastchester, near Yonkers ten miles to the south, then in 1806 he sold it and moved with his family upstate to the town of Broome in Schoharie County. Paulding settled on a farm at VanCortlandville near Peekskill, thirty miles to the north of Tarrytown.

Alexander Hamilton in an article written a week after Andre's death about the Arnold treason plot highly praises the three captors. Their exemplary conduct, he says, measured against that of the traitor affords a striking contrast in personal integrity. "While Arnold is handed down with execration to future times," he wrote, "posterity will repeat with reverence the names of Van Wart, Paulding, and Williams."

For thirty-seven years that just and generous sentiment held true, no one thinking to question or diminish it. Then suddenly, unexpectedly, in the spring of 1817 came Andre's revenge on his captors. Ever since, posterity's view of them has been sorely unsettled—gratitude and a measure of reverence, yes, but strangely mixed with rejection and disdain.

A few observers before this have suspected Andre's hand in the disturbing alteration but without pinning it to fact and circumstance. One of the more outspoken was a speaker at the dedication of a monument to David Williams at Schoharie in 1876. What Andre said about his three captors, stated Grenville Tremain of Albany, "sprang from a heart sorely dejected, chagrined, and mortified by his own lack of common prudence, when his mind was sunk beneath a weight of woe almost incalculable and was seeking for relief in the contemplation of what might have been." Andre's testimony about his captors, finished Tremain, was wholly spurious and arose out of "a cauldron of self-interest."

Other nineteenth-century commentators put it more directly, charging that "Andre left as a legacy a blow at his captors," or that he consciously and deliberately sought to "revenge his failure by stabbing the character and blackening the fame of his captors."

Despite all his calculation, exactly how it was to be done Andre could never have foreseen. But he chose his instrument very well indeed.

AFTER THE WAR, BEN TALLMADGE returned to his home in Litchfield, Connecticut, where he married, began a family that would eventually include five sons and two daughters, and prospered in business. He then entered politics and in 1800 was elected to the first of six terms in the House of Representatives. His reputation as a military man never faded, however, and in 1793 when war with France seemed a possibility and the army was to be expanded, he was personally marked by Washington for a top command in the U.S. cavalry. That particular war scare passed, but again at the start of the War of 1812 he was offered a high command, this time by President Madison, which he declined.

Though as a Federalist in politics he had his political enemies, among his colleagues in the halls of Congress his personal prestige was high. Whenever he spoke his views commanded wide attention, particularly if the topic concerned the men and events of Revolutionary times. A reserved, physically large man, he had "a military and austere appearance" which reminded people of Washington. His neighbors in Litchfield were inclined to look on him as "some godlike creature from another world" and time. By 1817, of the storied figures remaining in the House from the Revolution, he was by far the most conspicuous. Few of his fellow representatives, in fact, had any clear, personal memories of that life-and-death struggle. It was a different generation.

While Ben Tallmadge was steadily making his way up in the business world and in Congress, John Paulding was content to run his farm while fathering an ever-increasing family, eventually producing twenty-one children by three wives. Married first in 1784 to Sarah Teed (or Tidd) of Peekskill, his first three children were girls, one of whom died in infancy. His first son, born in 1789, he named George Washington Paulding (he too died in infancy). That same year in October his wife died of an illness, and in November 1790 Paulding remarried, choosing another Peekskill girl, Esther Ward. During the next twelve years Esther gave birth to eight children, three of them girls. One of the five boys was given the name of the deceased son, George Washington Paulding. Another son, Hiram, as a boy of fourteen, through his father's influence was appointed by President Madison a midshipman in the U.S. Navy (eventually after fifty years of important service reaching the rank of rear admiral).

In 1804 Esther died (perhaps in childbirth), and after another year Paulding again married, a young woman named Hester Denike. By the fall of 1816 Paulding was the father of seven more children, giving him a total at that time of seventeen living offspring, eight of them girls. The oldest was a girl, Nancy, aged thirty. Youngest was a boy, Samuel, only a year old. It was the care of this large family, along with his increasing physical disability (perhaps a result of the bayonet wound), that led him to ask Congress for an increase in the $200 annual pension awarded the captors nearly forty years before. Another legitimate reason, of course, was the loss of purchasing power over the years. By then the original $200 had lost about half its value.

Paulding's petition, prepared with the help of a local lawyer, was submitted late in 1816. Two months later came the decision of the House Committee on Pensions, a not really surprising negative. The topic of military pensions for Revolutionary War soldiers and those from the just concluded War of 1812 was a troubled one in those early years, much contested, and the House Committee viewed Paulding's request as dangerously precedent-setting. Its formal report, dated January 13, 1817, deserves to be read almost entire. After identifying Paulding as one of Andre's captors and mentioning Washington's personal "approbation" and the two hundred dollar annuity, the report goes on:

> He states that he is now old, has a large family, some of whom are infants; that he is very infirm, and incapable of hard labor; that his annuity is his greatest dependance to maintain himself and family; and asks Congress to increase the allowance which he now has, or to grant him such further assistance as his faithful and patriotic services, and his infirmity and advanced age, may demand.
>
> The petitioner did his duty faithfully, and for it he has been liberally rewarded. However, he did nothing more than his duty; the country expects this much, at least, from everyone, and yet it is not expected that she is to support all who have done so. The Committee, without disparaging the services of the petitioner, can conceive of many individuals, both in the Revolutionary and late war, who rendered services of the highest character, if not equal to those of the petitioner, and who, so far from being so highly favored with the public liberality as he has been, have received nothing, and who have asked nothing.
>
> Good policy warns us against adopting such measures as may excite invidious remarks and create jealousies.

The petitioner was a private soldier when he rendered the services for which he had been thus liberally rewarded; he was neither wounded nor in any way injured,* nor even exposed to a greater degree of hardship than thousands of soldiers who were then in service; and yet for those brave men who then fought our battles, and who had the misfortune to lose an arm or a leg, or who became otherwise wounded or disabled, and who have dragged out a tardy and melancholy and perhaps miserable existence, no greater provision was made than an allowance of sixty dollars per year, until the last session of Congress, when it was increased to ninety-six.

His provision was a far more liberal one. He does not now suggest that his annuity is not sufficient to support himself; but he wishes out of the public bounty to support himself and his family too. This is a request which is not granted to those who were disabled in the service of the country, nor to the widows and orphans of those who were slain. It can therefore hardly be proper to grant it to the petitioner. He has no cause of complaint against the government, and ought to be satisfied; therefore,

Resolved, That the prayer of the petitioner is unreasonable, and ought not to be granted.

But the decision met strong opposition from a large group of Congressmen who thought that Paulding's request was not at all "unreasonable," in view of what he'd done forty years before. As the official House record, *The Annals of Congress*, puts it, "A debate of no little interest arose on this question," with Paulding's supporters insisting on the unique importance of his service, his faithfulness to duty in

---

*Strangely, this overlooks the bayonet wound or wounds sustained by Paulding in his last action against the British in Westchester, in which he was captured. See p. 155 and the Notes.

the face of temptation, and the need to allow for "the depreciation of money" since the granting of the pension originally.

Speakers opposing the request dwelt on the points made in the report, mainly that it would be wrong to legislate "on a single case" for pension increase, especially while there were many other old soldiers "languishing in obscurity and want; to whom no relief had been or would be granted."

It was at this juncture that Ben Tallmadge rose in the House to speak on the question. What he said that day—"on the authority of Major Andre"—about the three captors introduced a seriously jarring note into the debate which greatly surprised the listening members, and which many of them felt to be both unnecessary and inappropriate. Apparently fearing that the pension increase for Paulding would carry despite the Committee report, he attempted to put the question on a different basis, whether or not Paulding was in fact *worthy* of such added help, whether his motive in the "unique" service was really so patriotic as had always been believed. The words he uttered in the House on that occasion became a permanent part of the public record, and ever since among a certain class of historians have echoed in condemnation of all three captors.

Let the official account from the congressional *Annals* tell the curious story:

> What gave interest principally to the debate was the disclosure by Mr. Tallmadge of Connecticut (an officer at the time, and commanding the advance guard when Major Andre was brought in) of his view of the merit of this transaction, with which history and the records of the country have made every man familiar.
>
> The value of the service he did not deny, but on the authority of the declarations of Major Andre (made while in the custody of Col. Tallmadge) he gave it as his opinion that, if Major Andre could have given to these men the amount they demanded for his release, he never would have been hung for

a spy, nor in captivity on that occasion. Mr. T.'s statement was minutely circumstantial, and given with expressions of his individual confidence of its correctness. Among other circumstances, he stated, that when Major Andre's boots were taken off by them, it was to search for plunder, and not to detect treason.

These persons indeed, he said, were of that class of people who passed between both armies, as often in one camp as the other, and whom, he said, if he had met with them, he should probably as soon have apprehended as Major Andre, as he had always made it a rule to do with these suspicious persons.

The conclusion to be drawn from the whole of Mr. Tallmadge's statement, of which this is a brief extract, was that these persons had brought in Major Andre only because they should probably get more for his apprehension than for his release.

The speech drew strong public reaction, especially in newspaper comment, much of which condemned Tallmadge's assertions as lacking all historical basis. The Congressman's ill-advised accusation, observed the New York *Evening Post*, "has drawn down much reproach upon that gentleman from various quarters."

Angry editorials were plentiful. One indignant effort in the New York *Courier* reported incredulously that the Tallmadge speech "ventured to ascribe to the celebrated captors of Andre a character the most infamous and detestable, and to their conduct on that occasion motives the most sordid and odious . . . he charged them, in effect, with being the vilest of thieves and robbers . . . not from his own knowledge but from the calumnies of the envious and the mere suspicions of an enemy." What were Tallmadge's grounds for the accusation? asked the *Courier*:

Did he know the facts? If he did he must have seen them steal; he must have seen them in the enemy's camp: But he does not pretend this. What then is the evidence of these facts? At the most hearsay . . . the utmost that can be said in palliation of Col. Tallmadge's conduct is that he believed what he said to be true. He believed [the captors] to be cow-boy plunderers because he *heard* so . . . because Andre *said* he was of that opinion! . . . there is not a court in Christendom which would not spurn such evidence . . .

Colonel Tallmadge, thought the *Courier*, in his unfortunate remarks on the House floor, had displayed "a rashness which he will never cease to repent."

In the House itself a staunch rebuttal immediately followed on Tallmadge concluding his remarks. As the congressional *Annals* noted, the charges against the captors were

. . . received with surprise and incredulity, as to Major Andre's correctness, by the gentlemen on the other side of this question. It was very extraordinary, it was said, that at a day so much nearer the transaction than the present, there had existed no doubt on the subject, and Congress, as a mark of public gratitude for their honorable conduct on this important occasion, settled on these persons pensions for life.

Though testimony was strongly stated by one of the gentlemen (Mr. Smith) to Major Andre's high character and honor, it was impossible, it was said, that the character and conduct of the men should have been as this day represented, yet so differently depicted.

The statement of Major Andre, subject as it must have been to be discolored by misapprehensions of the character and motives of Americans, among whom patriotism pervades every rank in life, it was urged, ought to have no weight, indeed it ought not to have been mentioned, in competition with the facts on record, and established by full investigation during the lifetime of General Washington, who certainly knew all the circumstances of the transaction . . .

Several motions followed, one defiantly increasing not only Paulding's pension but those of Williams and Van Wart as well ("which motion was negatived"). Another sought to postpone a decision on the question in order to "examine," presumably in a full-blown committee hearing, the truth of Tallmadge's accusation. This was offered by a member who indignantly declared himself a believer in the captors' "pure and incorruptible" motives. It too was denied.

After all the excitement had died down an immediate vote was called for. It was taken and the original report of the Pension Committee was upheld (and Paulding's petition rejected) by a vote of fifty-three to eighty. The majority simply decided that approval of this "single case" would open the door for a flood of such petitions. In the end, Tallmadge's speech had no effect whatever on the Paulding petition. It would have been defeated if he'd never opened his mouth, never recalled what Andre had said to him forty years before.

Was it really only out of a desire to thwart Paulding's request that he'd taken the drastic step of overturning the country's long-held belief about the captors, by then almost legendary? Could he, nearly four decades afterward, still be so keenly conscious of his sorrow over Andre's death, still feel the old anguish that so marvelous a youth had to die? The answer is found in a letter Tallmadge wrote to the historian Jared Sparks long after that contentious day in the House of Representatives. Telling of his association with Andre in the days before his execution, he confesses that he still can hardly bear to think or write about the tragic event: "Give me leave to remark that so deeply were my feelings interested in the fate of this unfortunate young Man, that I believe I have never narrated the story, nor perused the account of his merited, but ignominious death without shedding tears of sorrow over such blighted prospects. I hope and trust this will be the last trial of my feelings in this way." The date of the letter is 1833, less than two years before his death.

His only clearly stated reason for doing what he did in his House speech occurs in another letter, this one written five years after the fact (September 1822). "Knowing the circumstances which related to Major Andre," he says, "I felt it to be my duty to state some facts, that the House might act accordingly on the Occasion. This was all I attempted to do, & even then my remarks were sadly misrepresented . . . as to the Captors, I have no wish to detract from their merit in the public estimation, where no duty requires it; nor to wound their feelings, nor those of their friends in any degree."

It was a matter of "duty," then, a sense of obligation, that prompted his speech of condemnation in the House. But duty how, to what or to whom? To that question there's an inevadable answer, obvious though beyond proof. He is speaking of duty to the doomed Major Andre, who in some manner made it plain to the impressionable young American officer how he wanted the record of his capture to read (an event which he knew to his sorrow would be forever marked as the most egregious failure of nerve, of readiness and foresight, of mental balance and self-possession in the history of espionage). Why it took Tallmadge so long to do it, to put Andre's spurious claim on record, is another question hard to settle. Perhaps at first he himself had trouble fully believing what Andre told him. Perhaps he gave in only with the passing of time as the Englishman's gallant-seeming image year by year glowed brighter, bringing with it an ever more vivid reflection of Tallmadge's own lost youth.

The reaction of at least one of the captors to the Tallmadge charge was intense, expressed immediately and in public. No sooner did the fifty-eight-year-old Van Wart get wind of the slur cast on him and the other two captors than he took action. Promptly he swore out a formal affidavit rejecting the charge—and found himself supported in the action by a large crowd of his friends and neighbors who indignantly did the same. Both documents were presented to Congress, showing up in many newspapers as well. The New York *Evening Post* gave both with the comment that Van Wart's sworn word was at least as good as the unsworn, not to say sneaking testimony of Andre.

Understandably, what bothered Van Wart most was the imputation that he'd trafficked with both sides in the war, in other words was a member of some marauding band of freebooters, running now with the Cowboys and now with the Skinners. After lengthily detailing the circumstances of the capture, he states that the crestfallen Andre tried to bribe them,

> ... promised to make them any reward which they might name, if they would but permit him to proceed, which they refused. He then told them that if they doubted the fulfillment of his promise they might conceal him in some secret place and keep him there until they could send to New York and receive their reward. And this deponent expressly declares that every offer made by Major Andre to them was promptly and resolutely refused.
>
> ... And this deponent further says that he never visited the British camp, nor does he believe or suspect that either Paulding or Williams ever did, except that Paulding was once before Andre's capture, and once afterwards, made a prisoner by the British, as this deponent has been informed and believes.
>
> And this deponent for himself expressly denies that he ever held any unlawful traffic, or any intercourse whatever with the enemy. And—appealing solemnly to that omniscient Being at whose tribunal he must soon appear—he doth expressly declare that all accusations charging him therewith are utterly untrue.

The neighbors' affidavit was signed by no less than seventeen men ranging in age from thirty to nearly ninety, and bearing such respected Dutch names as Dyckman, Requa, Odell, and Van Tassel, all of them to be found on the rolls of the Westchester militia in the Revolution. The signers claimed acquaintance with all three captors and insisted that at no time during the Revolution "was a suspicion entertained by their neighbors or acquaintances that they or either of them held any undue intercourse with the enemy. On the contrary, they were universally esteemed and taken to be ardent and faithful in the cause of the country." Of Van Wart himself the signers declare that "there is not an individual in the County of Westchester, acquainted with Isaac Van Wart, who would hesitate to describe him as a man whose integrity is as unimpeachable as his veracity is undoubted."

Paulding also responded in a sworn affidavit, though for some reason it didn't reach Congress or the newspapers until May. Making no reference to the Tallmadge speech, it concentrates on supplying a clear account of the immediate monetary award given to the captors, as provided by Westchester's then law of contraband:

> ... among other articles which they took from Major Andre were his watch, horse, saddle and bridle, and which they retained as prize ... that shortly thereafter they were summoned to appear as witnesses at the headquarters of General Washington at Tappan ... that while there Col. William S. Smith redeemed the watch from them for thirty guineas, which, and the money received for the horse, saddle and bridle, they divided equally among themselves and four other persons who belonged to their party, but when Andre was taken were about half a mile off keeping a look-out on a hill; that Andre had no gold or silver money with him, but only some continental bills to the amount of about eighty dollars ...

In the years immediately after the Tallmadge attack, historians vigorously defended the captors, some not hesitating to question Tallmadge's competence in the matter (though allowing him full credit for his own valuable and even heroic military service). "I shall not further notice the attempt to take from the captors of Major Andre," wrote Alexander Garden in 1822 in his widely read book, *Anecdotes of the Revolutionary War*, "the credit so justly acquired by their refusing the bribes which he offered, than to express my satisfaction at its complete failure . . . Fascinated by the manners and character of Major Andre, and particularly by the firmness he displayed, it is evident that Major Tallmadge was prepared to believe whatever he might assert." It was a shrewd guess of Garden's, laying Tallmadge's words to the direct influence of Andre, and it was made without benefit of the several candid comments made later by Tallmadge as to Andre's strong personal influence on him.

Unfortunately, Garden's prediction about the "complete failure" of the attack all too soon proved wrong. With Tallmadge's stark declaration spread permanently on the record, the damage was done. Never afterwards would the names of the captors be entirely free from strong suspicion of cupidity, rising at times to outright condemnation. In books and articles on the Revolution, on Washington, on the Arnold treason plot, on Andre himself, the three might be lauded as staunch patriots but might equally be dismissed as unworthy of their heroic roles, patriots by accident. Blithely, seldom stopping to identify or discuss the basis of their choices, different authors would adopt one or the other verdict, embellishing it as they wished.

Gradually it became acceptable for a writer to favor any shade of opinion about the captors, from ringing praise to flat repudiation. The reality, the truth of the matter no longer seemed reason for delay in telling the old story. The three captors were either great-spirited men of honor and integrity, or they were—in the words of a more recent, well-received biography of Benedict Arnold—nothing but "common highwaymen" prowling the countryside in search of plunder, "three of the blackest villains of the era, who just happened to stop the right man at the right time."

One comprehensive 1976 reference work, *Who Was Who During*

The Captors' monument at Tarrytown, New York, commemorating the site of the capture.

The Paulding monument standing over his grave in the cemetery of St. Peter's Church, VanCortlandville, New York (North Peekskill).

the Revolution, has NO mention of the captors! A similar 1993 volume, *Who Was Who in the Revolution*, lists all three but styles them "a rather scruffy lot," marauders who were in search only of "booty" and who found the papers by accident. The same volume pictures Andre as a "romantic" figure whose wonderful "nobility and forebearance" when facing his doom won the affection of all.

One year after the rejection of the original Paulding pension request by the House in 1817, the old patriot grew ill and, surrounded by his family, he died on his farm near Peekskill. The news of his passing was widely reported, though the obituaries, in keeping with the practice of the times, were rather short. An eight-line notice in the *National Intelligencer* in Washington called him "one of the three incorruptible patriots who arrested Major Andre during the Revolutionary War." The New York *Spectator* gave him his rank (honorary) in the Westchester militia, Major John Paulding, but without a mention of the deed that brought him fame, assuming that readers would know who it was (that was true up to the close of the nineteenth century).

Curiously, the news of his passing brought from Ben Tallmadge an unexpected, apparently contrite reaction. Reversing himself on the matter of the pension, he introduced a motion in the House to continue it indefinitely for the benefit of the widow and her many children. The motion was denied.

A LARGE CROWD OF MOURNERS including many of the area's notables overflowed snow-covered St. Peter's Cemetery at Cortlandville, New York, when John Paulding was laid to rest on February 20, 1818. Among the speakers was Isaac Van Wart, who told feelingly of his old comrade. Near the grave in two ranks stood twenty West Point cadets freezing in the cold but splendidly attired in dress uniforms. At the service's end they lifted their muskets and fired three volleys in a last salute. One of the cadets was a young man named George Washington Tallmadge, eighteen-year-old son of Ben. The coincidence was "somewhat singular," thought his father.

Ten years later in the cemetery of the Dutch Reformed Church at Elmsford, New York, Isaac Van Wart was buried. As with Paulding, a large crowd of neighbors, friends, and notables was on hand. Lining the gravesite were his widow, three of his four children, and several grandchildren. The services were conducted by Isaac's son, the Reverend Alexander Van Wart. At their conclusion another contingent of twenty West Point cadets fired the last salute.

David Williams had three years in which to bask in the role of sole surviving captor. When New York City in the fall of 1830 planned a citywide festival in recognition of France's role in the Revolution, and to commemorate France's own 1789 Revolution, Williams was one of the honored guests. It was also the fiftieth anniversary of Andre's capture, and to mark the event in the elaborate grand parade Williams rode in a special carriage at the head of the Revolutionary War veterans. The festival lasted a week with Williams being honored at several ceremonial dinners and banquets. The city's schoolchildren gave him a silver cup, and another group presented him with a silver-headed cane made from a West Point oak. The experience was an emotional one for the aged veteran, once or twice bringing tears to his eyes. Still, at a gala ball in his honor, "the old soldier entered into the amusement with great spirit, and was not behind any of the gentlemen present in his gallantry to the ladies. When the Scotch reels were introduced he could scarcely refrain from taking the floor and leading the dance."

The place to take leave of this last of the captors, eight months before his death on August 2, 1831, is in the audience at New York's Bowery Theater as the festival closes. Before an enthusiastic audience unfolds a play called *The Glory of Columbia*, written in 1803 by the prominent early American playwright, William Dunlap. Integral to the exciting story was a scene depicting the capture of Major Andre, in which all three captors have speaking parts. When the young actor playing Williams delivered his opening lines, he paused, came forward to the footlights, and introduced the real David Williams seated in the first row.

Responding to the wildly cheering house, the seventy-six-year-old Williams, "quite overcome with emotion," rose to his feet, waved to all sides, then gave a stiff little bow. Perhaps in that audience there were some older members able to picture on either side of Williams the smiling ghosts of Paulding and Van Wart, all three graciously bowing.

EPILOGUE: LOOSE ENDS

I n America today there stand in testimony to the foiling of the
Arnold treason plot four different monuments, none very large.
Three mark the graves of the captors, the fourth, and largest after
receiving an addition in 1880, commemorates the capture site at
Tarrytown, standing near but not on the actual spot, now well within
city limits.

The monument on Paulding's grave went up first, but not until
ten years after his death, and it took an influential relative in government to accomplish it. In 1826, a nephew of Paulding's, William
Paulding, was elected mayor of New York City. Next year the city
fathers voted to erect an appropriate marker on John's grave, a granite
shaft properly inscribed. At the dedication ceremony in November
1827 Mayor William Paulding traveled upriver to the cemetery at
VanCortlandville to give the main address. A number of generals
were also on hand along with a crowd of the area's notables. Isaac
Van Wart was there too to tell the old story of the capture in public
one last time. When, six months later Van Wart himself died, his
grave had to wait only a year for its monument. On June 11, 1829,
with a large crowd and appropriate ceremony, a tall granite shaft was
erected by the citizens of Westchester.

David Williams's grave waited the longest for a fitting memorial, and to accomplish it his remains had to be moved to a new location. Buried first, in August 1831, at Livingstonville, forty-five years later the body was exhumed and transported to Schoharie to be given a place of honor in the Old Stone Fort, a Revolutionary relic. As the coffin, covered by a large American flag, passed through the town in July 1876, all businesses were closed, and "all the bells of the churches, and of the Academy and the Court House, were tolled, and the cannon at the Fort were fired in a salute." Three months later, on September 29 before an audience of ten thousand, amid speeches, cannon salutes, and the reading of a specially commissioned, 150-line commemorative poem, with the town sporting "a splendid lot of bunting," and "festooned arches and floral decorations," the new monument to David Williams was dedicated.

A shaft of Massachusetts marble on a stepped pedestal, it stands almost twenty-five feet high. The inscription reads:

Here rest the remains of
DAVID WILLIAMS
One of the captors of
Major Andre,
Died in Schoharie County
Aug. 2d, 1831,
Aged 76 years, 6 mos., 8 days

He with his compatriots John Paulding and Isaac Van Wart, on the 23rd of September, 1780, arrested Major John Andre and found on his person treasonable papers in the handwriting of General Benedict Arnold, who sought by treachery to surrender the military post of West Point into the hands of the enemy. In resisting the great bribes of their prisoner for his liberty, they showed their incorruptible patriotism, the American Army was saved, and our beloved Country became free.

The captors' monument at Tarrytown, marking the site of the capture, was put up in two stages, the second stage being a happy afterthought. The original monument, a marble obelisk, went up in 1853, with many descendents and relatives of the captors in attendance at the dedication ceremony. Then in 1880, as part of the celebration of the hundredth anniversary of the capture, a bronze statue was added atop the original shaft, a near-life-size figure of John Paulding. Chairman of the occasion was Samuel L. Tilden, recently defeated Democratic candidate for U.S. president. The orator of the day was the nationally known New York politician Chauncey M. Depew. A member of the committee was Paulding's son, Rear-Admiral Hiram Paulding, then retired.

Other children and grandchildren of the three captors were also present in 1880, including the Reverend Alexander Van Wart, Isaac's son, who gave the blessing. He caused unexpected tears to flow when he ended his invocation with a mention of Andre himself. "Help us so to live that when our account shall be settled up," he prayed, "we may leave a record behind us to our friends who survive us, that they will have no cause to be ashamed of us, and if we should be so happy, Heavenly Father, as to be permitted to enter the gates of pearl into the City of the Living God, it would be a great pleasure to us to meet Major Andre there, a happy and a glorified saint in Heaven."

From time to time over the years efforts have been made to have the federal government fund a large, prominent monument in Washington D.C., commemorating the capture of Andre and nationally honoring the captors. All have failed.

IN ADDITION TO THE MONUMENT in Westminster Abbey, Andre's memory was preserved and honored in two other ways, the official approbation of his king and in verse by his literary friends.

In Bath lived Andre's family, his mother and her three unmarried daughters. To the mother soon after her son's death the king sent a gift of a thousand guineas, then settled on her an annual pension of three hundred pounds, with right of reversion to her daughters (the last of the family, Mary, died in 1845). The king also gave to Andre's brother William the recognition that would have gone to the dead man, creating him a baronet.

The writing of obituary and commemorative verse was a widespread practice of the time, and Andre's sad fate was perfectly calculated to call forth any number of such attempts. The only effort that rose even a little above the commonplace was a long (460 lines in rhymed couplets) "Monody on the Death of Major Andre," written by an established poet who had known Andre as one of the Litchfield literary circle, Anna Seward.

Briefly telling Andre's story in a curiously allusive manner, replete with the personifications, exhortations, and elaborate apostrophes seemingly inevitable in eighteenth-century verse, the poem is not memorable, though in its day it gained some attention. The frenetic opening lines are meant only to record the news of the major's death reaching England from America:

> Loud howls the storm! The vex'd Atlantic roars!
> Thy Genius, Briton, wanders on its shores!
> Hears cries of horror wafted from afar,
> And groans of Anguish mid the shrieks of war!
> Hears the deep curses of the Great and Brave
> Sigh in the wind and murmur on the Wave . . .

It was this composition that established the legend of Andre's thwarted love for Honora Sneyd, taking Andre's word for it (the sentimental Miss Seward was a close friend of Honora's and should have known better). More significantly, some scathing lines in the poem condemning Washington for some years distorted many Englishmen's estimate of the American general. Branding him a "cool, determined Murderer of the Brave," she predicts a like fate for Andre's implacable judge:

Remorseless Washington! The day shall come
Of deep repentance for this barb'rous doom!
When injured Andre's memory shall inspire
A kindling army with resistless fire;
Each falchion sharpen that the Britons wield,
And lead their fiercest Lion to the field!
Then, when each hope of thine shall set in night,
When dubious dread and unavailing flight
Impel your host, thy guilt-upbraided soul
Shall wish untouched the sacred life you stole!
And when thy heart appall'd and vanquished pride
Shall vainly ask the mercy they deny'd,
With horror shalt thou meet the fate they gave,
Nor Pity gild the darkness of thy grave!

She ends with a hope that the martyred soldier, his body then lying "Damp in the earth on Hudson's shore," will not be forgotten, but that

. . . its dust, like Abel's blood, shall rise
And call for justice from the angry skies!

To the lady's credit, on later learning more of the facts of the case she changed her mind about Washington's role and to some extent the justice of Andre's sentence.

HE NEVER KNEW IT, but Benedict Arnold came within a hair of falling into Washington's avenging hands and finishing his career at the end of a rope in a public hanging. When the negotiations for a trade of Andre for Arnold failed, Washington selected an intrepid sergeant-major from the army, a twenty-four-year-old Virginian named John Champe, and sent him into New York City with a mission to seize Arnold bodily and bring him out.

The plan was an elaborate one in which Champe apparently deserted his unit in New Jersey to join the new American Loyalist corps then forming under Arnold. Some three weeks after Andre's death, Champe reached New York, presented himself to the British command, and was unquestioningly assigned to serve under Arnold, whom he met face to face. With the help of two American spies already in the city he was to surprise Arnold in his garden at night, spirit him through darkened streets to a boat waiting on the Hudson shore, and row across the river to the American lines. At the critical moment, however, Arnold's corps was suddenly ordered south, and Champe could not avoid going with it.

After that, one or two other kidnap attempts were made, but all failed. As long as the traitor continued as a British officer leading troops in America, Washington never gave up hope of making him pay with his life for his treason. All Washington's combat generals and other high officers had standing orders that if Arnold were ever taken alive in battle he was to be summarily hanged. But Arnold escaped his former Chief's wrath and after the war returned to England, where he died in 1801.

WHETHER THE ENIGMATIC MAN who served as Andre's host and guide, Joshua Hett Smith, was criminally culpable in the treason affair has never been quite settled. His trial for treason, for two weeks in October 1780 before the regular court-martial board of the army, ended in a finding of "insufficient evidence" and an acquittal. Almost everyone at the time, however, was convinced of his guilt, including Washington, convinced that he had full knowledge of and willingly aided Arnold's traitorous designs. To later generations his role in the affair seems quite subordinate, not mattering much whether he was guilty or innocent. In the end most observers tended to see him as a willing dupe, knowing much of the truth and easily able to guess more, though ignorant of Arnold's ultimate intention to sacrifice West Point and its body of troops. In what Smith wrote later on the point there is much force of reason: "I will here request the candid and liberal reader to judge whether any man in his senses would or would not have refused to carry Mr. Anderson back to the *Vulture*, if he knew the extent of General Arnold's plot, and the danger to which he was exposed in case of a discovery."

If Smith had in fact been an integral part of the plot or privy to the full reality of it, he would surely have found a way to *immediately* deliver Andre back aboard the *Vulture* at the conclusion of the meeting with Arnold on the shore. Or if not that night, then surely the next night. He would never have risked that long journey by horse down through Westchester. That the decision to return Andre to the ship by land was in fact made by Smith is established by the available testimony.

Though there was not enough evidence to convict Smith at his army trial, his acquittal did not bring him release. Instead, he was turned over to the state's civilian authority to await another trial. It never came to that. With outside help he managed to escape from the loosely guarded jail, soon after leaving the country for England. Living there for some thirty years, he kept in touch with his large family in America (his four children, a dozen brothers and sisters of his own, and any number of grandchildren, nephews, and nieces). Eventually he returned to America, living obscurely in New York City. His death came in the same year as that of John Paulding, 1818.

Reading the newspaper obituaries of Paulding and the accounts of his funeral full of lavish praise of the old patriot, Smith's last days were heavy with thoughts of what might have been. Especially he could not have escaped thinking how different it would have all turned out if, instead of leaving Andre to proceed alone at Pines Bridge, he had accompanied him all the way into the city. That simple, still unexplained decision saved him two or so further hours of horseback riding and lost a world.

INSPIRED BY HIS FATHER'S FAMOUS EXAMPLE with a thirst for military glory, Hiram Paulding as an officer in the U.S. Navy enjoyed a brilliant fifty-year career, capping it in 1857 with a sensational capture of his own. Like his father's exploit with Andre, it brought him both high praise and rejection and sparked a debate in Congress. It also forced him into temporary retirement.

It was Commodore Paulding who put an end to the filibustering expedition of the adventurous William Walker in Central America. But to do it he had to exceed his authority, and he paid for his daring. Only the coming of the Civil War rescued his career. As the father met and was honored by Washington, so the son met and was honored by President Lincoln.

In the 1850s Central America was the focus of a bewildering array of interests, both American and British (the British acting in blithe defiance of the Monroe Doctrine), all focusing on the dream of linking the two great oceans by a canal. Complicating matters were the South's desire for the expansion of slavery (with covetous eyes on Cuba as well), the hopes of American capitalists for controlling the area's development, and the yearning of the poor peons to break the hold of feudal serfdom. Offering a volatile mixture of politics, economics, idealism, and national pride—that intense belief in what was called "manifest destiny"—the region was a magnet for the ambitious and the adventurous. At that time the route favored for the inter-ocean canal was Nicaragua, not Panama, and here in 1856 appeared the charismatic adventurer who for years would dominate the scene, William Walker.

At the head of a small private army recruited in the United States, supposedly at the urging of its democratic element, Walker invaded Nicaragua, fought several battles against huge odds, and made himself master of the country. His exploits and personality, and his policies as the duly elected president of Nicaragua, brought him worldwide fame and made him a favorite with the American public. But he had violated America's neutrality laws (no private military interference in the affairs of friendly nations), and to an extent the Clayton–Bulwer Treaty with England (neither country may attempt to dominate the region), and it was reluctantly decided that he had to be chastened. President Buchanan sent a squadron of U.S. naval ships, under Commodore Paulding, to demand that Walker and his army vacate the country, arriving on Nicaragua's east coast late in 1857.

Paulding had been given no specific orders on what to do if Walker refused, but when he did refuse, the son of old John Paulding didn't hesitate.

With Walker's force encamped at a coastal town, Paulding drew his five ships up abreast then leveled all his guns at the unprotected buildings. Putting three hundred marines ashore, he sent them in a circling move to Walker's rear, cutting off any hope of a retreat into the interior. His second in command he sent ashore with a note to Walker demanding immediate surrender. As a sign of compliance the Nicaraguan flag was to be lowered. Within minutes of Walker reading the note, the flag came down.

Back in America the incident caused a sensation. Praise for Commodore Paulding's decisive independent action was widespread and unstinted. But those who condemned his threat of force against a "foreign power" were equally loud, both sides being swayed by the politics of the moment. In Congress a heated debate erupted and at one point this exchange occurred:

Rep. John Haskin (New York): Now, Sir, who is Commodore Paulding, a constituent of mine of whom I am justly proud? He is the son of that John Paulding of Revolutionary memory, who with Williams and Van Wart, captured Major Andre near Sleepy Hollow, Westchester County—a spot with which I am as familiar as I am with this Hall . . . Mr. Chairman, John Paulding, the father of Commodore Paulding, had no *search warrant*, no special directions from the government to do what he did. He had no orders from the Continental Congress directing him to search and arrest Andre . . .

Rep. John Cochrane (New York): Will my colleague allow me to ask him a question? I ask whether this spirit of committing offenses against the law of nations runs in the family?

Mr. Haskin: If my colleague considered such [to be] an

offense against the law of nations, then I admit it runs in the blood. I was, Mr. Chairman, merely giving the history of Paulding, the captor of Andre, to prove that Commodore Paulding was the worthy son of a patriotic sire, and I insist that he has better reason to be proud of his ancestor than any monarch seated on any of the thrones of Europe . . . In reference to this act of Commodore Paulding in arresting Walker, I believe that no other act since the inauguration of the existing administration has reflected more honor and credit upon the country, and I sincerely trust that the responsible majority of this House will not fritter away that honor and credit by any resolution of censure against Commodore Paulding.

No censure was voted, but he was quietly relieved of his command (the prestigious Home Squadron), and soon afterward at age sixty-one he retired from the service. For three years he remained at home with his wife and younger children, running his hundred-acre farm at Huntington, Long Island. With the coming of the Civil War he was called back to Washington and given a series of important departmental assignments, deliberately being kept from any command at sea. Even in that situation he managed to accomplish work of signal importance. He was one of those mainly responsible for the building of the ironclad *Monitor*, and for having it ready in time to meet, and defeat, the dire threat of the South's *Merrimac* at Hampton Roads.

His meeting with Lincoln—actually several meetings—occurred in the course of his duties as commander of the strategically important New York Navy Yard, to which he'd been personally appointed by President Lincoln, and in his role as special assistant to the Secretary of the Navy.

THE LENGTHIEST, MOST INTENSE, and technically involved discussion of Andre's status, whether spy or not, was kicked off seventy-five

years after the fact by Lord Mahon's *History of England* (vol. VII,
1855). Deciding in favor of Andre, seeing him as acting legitimately
as a soldier according to the law of nations, the influential Mahon
judged Andre's death to be "by far the greatest if perhaps the only
blot" on Washington's character. His opponents, of course all Americans, took a decidedly opposite view. The many pointless subtleties
and willful assumptions offered by Mahon were readily answered, and
today the exchange affords an interesting illustration of the whole
original, earnest, self-deluding argument.

In a ten-page rehearsal of the treason affair, Mahon begins by
quietly softening Andre's culpability. He was "prevailed upon" to enter American lines. His return to the *Vulture* after meeting Arnold
was thwarted because "the boatmen demurred and refused to convey
him." He changed into civilian clothes because he was "prevailed
upon" to do so. He carried the six incriminating documents because
he was "induced" to accept them. Most unfair, according to Mahon,
and even "inhumane," was the court's prompt acceptance of Andre's
confessional letter to Washington, "an avowal made with not a friend
or counsel beside him, and in the presence only of his bitterest foes."

The fourteen judges at the Court of Inquiry also drew heavy fire
from Mahon. They were, he declared roundly, simply unfit for their
demanding task:

> . . . it must be borne in mind that the American generals at
> that time were, for the most part, wholly destitute of the ad-
> vantages of a liberal education. They were men drawn from
> the plough-handle or the shop-board, at their country's call.
> Greene himself, the President of the Tribunal, had been a
> blacksmith by trade. These humble avocations afford no reason
> why such men might not always do their duty as became them
> in the field . . . But they do afford a reason, and as it seems to
> me a strong one, why such men, having no light of study to
> guide them, having probably never so much as heard the names

of Vattel or Puffendorf, could be no fit judges on any nice or doubtful point of national law . . . It follows then that the verdict of such a Tribunal ought to have no weight in such a case.

It is on the pass given by Arnold to Andre, in the name of Mr. Anderson, that Mahon rests his case. In truth, no more blatant or surprising instance of word-juggling can be found in the many discussions of the Andre affair:

> When Andre was arrested he was travelling under the protection of a pass which Arnold, as the commander of the West Point district, had a right to give. The Americans contend that this right was forfeited, or rendered of no effect, by Arnold's treacherous designs. Yet how hard to reconcile such a distinction with plighted faith and public law!
>
> How can we draw the line and say at what precise point the passes are to grow invalid—whether, when the treachery is in progress of execution, or when only matured in the mind, or when the mind is still wavering upon it? In short, how loose and slippery becomes the ground if once we forsake the settled principle of recognizing the safe-conducts granted by adequate authority, if once we stray forth in quest of secret motives and designs!

Among the many replies to Mahon, an eighty-page effort by Charles Biddle takes up the accusation of judicial incompetence. One by one, Biddle goes through the list of fourteen generals, laying out their backgrounds and finally showing the entire fitness of each for his position on the court. He also analyzes the application to the Andre case of the legal authorities Vattel and Puffendorf, finding the first to be inapplicable and the second to be in full support of the Andre court's decision. The question of the pass supplied by Arnold he analyzes in detail, showing the absurdity of the Americans being, under any interpretation, bound by a document intended to work their destruction.

A writer in the *North American Review* perhaps put it best. Mahon's argument supporting the validity of Arnold's pass, he suggests, "amounts simply to this. Arnold as commander of the West Point district, had a right to surrender the post; and to interfere with any contract or engagements which he made to that effect was wrong." The same writer concludes:

> All laws which are not based on common sense are common nuisances. Tested by this standard, we cannot conceive that the justice and lawfulness of Andre's fate should be generally and seriously questioned. His success was intended to be the ruin of America and the destruction of her leaders. What then should have been the penalty of his failure? It was a game of life and death . . . We therefore repeat what we believe is and ever will be the solemn conviction of our countrymen, if not of all the world, that his life was forfeited by his conduct, and that his death was just and necessary.

Of course, little or nothing was settled by the Mahon debate. Fifty years later *The English Historical Review* published a lengthy article covering much the same ground as had Lord Mahon and his predecessors, but with the old argument placed, as it promised, in "a new light." In part this added light proved to be still another new theory, quite seriously offered. In ordering a trial for Andre, charged the article, the stern and vengeful Washington had actually rigged the proceedings. Above all else, it seems, he wanted a conviction and a death sentence, giving him critical leverage in dealing with the English for the return of the hated Benedict Arnold.

ANDRE'S PERSONAL PARTICIPATION in the massacres of American troops at Paoli and Old Tappan became generally known only with the discovery of his diary in 1901. Found in England among the papers of his commander at the time, General "No-Flint" Grey, it was published soon after, documenting Andre's presence as Grey's aide at both locations. Before that, Andre's service with Grey had received little notice.

Winthrop Sargent in his 1860 biography of Andre recorded the Paoli incident, not as the massacre it was but as a regular part of the British 1778 campaign in New Jersey. His twenty-line account states coolly that the surprised Americans were "unable to form, and struggling irregularly or not at all, were instantly bayonetted. Our accounts put the killed and wounded at 150; the English version says 300 and upwards." Sargent also mentions the "action" at Old Tappan, in which Baylor's dragoons were slaughtered in their sleep or as they tried to surrender. But he ventures only that "Grey so skillfully led a night attack that the Americans had no opportunity of saving themselves, but by dispersion and flight. In affairs of this nature it is not the custom of war to lose time in receiving and disarming prisoners." As an afterthought he barely concedes that both Paoli and Old Tappan were "greatly censured in our camp and denounced" as massacres. But in neither case does he allow Andre's name to surface.

Sargent's tactic of downplaying the two massacres and Andre's part in them set the style for later writers during almost a century. Then J. T. Flexner in his 1953 volume, *The Traitor and the Spy*, made clear the awful reality of both incidents as well as Andre's participation. At Paoli,

> Andre heard steel piercing flesh, strangled death cries. In a few minutes several hundred men who were trying to flee were skewered, many of them, so patriots charged, after they had fallen on their knees to implore mercy. The wounded were given a second jab. Andre notes that about 200 were killed, forty seriously wounded, and only thirty-one captured not grievously hurt . . . even British participants dwelt on its "hor-

ror"; one regular considered it "altogether the most dreadful I ever beheld" . . .

Flexner also dug out of an old newspaper published in New York City during the Revolution an article written by Andre about Paoli. Grey's troops, wrote the then-Captain Andre, "put to the bayonet all they came up with and, overtaking the main herd of the fugitives, stabbed great numbers and pressed on their rear till it was thought prudent to order them to desist."

In 1967 the remains of some of Baylor's murdered men were accidentally unearthed in Old Tappan, the bones of six troopers who had been buried in makeshift graves. A regular archaeological dig was mounted, leading to a new historical study of the notorious incident and a renewed sense that—as General Lord Stirling said at the time—there never had been "a more determined Barbarous Massacre than they made of Baylor's Corps." When the results of the study were published in 1970 the map used to illustrate the movements of the British was one originally drawn by Captain John Andre and preserved in his diary. It showed Baylor's position at Old Tappan, labeled the "Rebel Dragoon cantonments," with lines indicating the British attack (the success of which, it might be noted, was made possible by information supplied to General Grey by a Tory spy in the neighborhood).

The same map also shows, a little to the northeast of the massacre site, just over the New York border, the town of Tappan where two years later Andre came to his own end.

NOTES AND SOURCES
SELECTED BIBLIOGRAPHY
ACKNOWLEDGEMENTS
INDEX

NOTES AND SOURCES

Along with source citations, these Notes offer a full discussion of every significant point in the narrative. Also included is a good deal of additional information which may be of interest or value. Citations of published sources are given in shortened form and may be identified by a glance at the bibliography.

The left-hand margin displays page numbers.

PROLOGUE: SOLDIER OR SPY?

1 "The noontide sun"—Child 169; the succeeding quotations from Child 171-83.

3 "a Star-Chamber proceeding"—Hendrickson 283.

4 "The character, appearance"—Irving V, 137. Same for the quotation in the next paragraph. But Irving had his own less favorable opinion of Andre: "Various circumstances connected with this nefarious negotiation argue lightness of mind and something of debasing alloy on the part of Andre." He meant that trafficking with a traitor was unsuitable for "a truly chivalrous nature" (102). At the time, of course, spying was seen as a necessary but utterly base part of warfare, not to be undertaken by a true soldier, an attitude shared by Andre himself.

4 "a peculiar elegance"—Hamilton 18. The description occurs in his long article on the Arnold treason affair written, probably at the request of

Washington, in October 1780. A lengthy production cast as a letter to a friend, it was meant to combat public misinformation and unrest, and was widely reprinted. Its praise of Andre was the first that the public had heard of the British officer.

4 "The fate of this unfortunate"—Quoted in Irving V, 148. The writer of the letter was Sir Thomas Romilly, who himself thought that the praise of Andre was "exaggerated." Mutius is a minor character in Shakespeare's *Titus Andronicus*, a young soldier slain by his own father, Titus. The application is not very clear.

5 "When all is spoken"—Sargent 499, 501.

6 "He was more unfortunate"—Fitzpatrick XX, 151.

7 "The interposition of"—Fitzpatrick XX, 132.

7 *Andre's background*: The fullest and most reliable sources for both the personal life and military detail are Hatch, Sargent, Randall, Van Doren, and Flexner. English sources are skimpier.

11 *The execution site today*: In Andre's time it was a wide-spreading, treeless field on a height overlooking Tappan and the Hudson River beyond. Now it is shrunk to a circular terminus of a dead-end road closely hemmed in by trees and private homes.

I: THE PRISONER

15 *Andre at Tappan*: Tallmadge 54-55; Stevens 253 (quoting an 1833 letter of Tallmadge; same in Sparks 256-59); Koke 129-32; Sargent 382-85; author's visits to site.

The Mabie Tavern is still in business, now called the Seventy-Six House. Until recently it featured a small, walled-off section of Andre's old prison-room containing a life-size wax figure of Andre seated at a table. The troop that delivered Andre to Tappan also brought his guide, Joshua Smith, who was imprisoned in a nearby church to await trial.

16 "apparent cheerfulness"—Greene 231. He adds that Andre is "a very accomplished character," and that while he condemns the spying, "cannot help pitying the man." Andre's trial, he says, will be "a disagreeable business but it must be done." This is hardly the supposed vengeful attitude attributed by English writers to Greene as head of the Court.

16 "I would wish the"—Fitzpatrick XX, 98.

17 *Board of Generals: Proceedings* 7 gives the original list of fourteen generals. Washington's choosing such a large tribunal to judge one man he

never explained, nor has anyone else. It shows at least how seriously
he viewed the entire treason affair, both in itself and as to its inevitable
public repercussions. Having more than twice as many judges as usual
did of course achieve a more balanced view of the case, reassuring
people on both sides.

18   "The most rigorous"—Fitzpatrick XX, 103.

20   "I never saw a man"—Webb 293, quotes Tallmadge to Webb.

20   "One of the most"—Sargent 531, quotes Tallmadge to Heath.

21   "I wished myself possessed"—Hendrickson 285.

21   *Andre's prior military service*: see above, 185-87, and below, 221-22.

21   "Coming in upon the"—Andre 49-50. The Paoli slaughter became a
rallying cry for Americans.

21   *Baylor Massacre*: For some detail see below, 221. Efforts by some commentators to obscure or explain away Andre's part in this and the kill-
ings at Paoli for a long time actually succeeded. They must now be
given their full weight in the Andre story.

21   "The whole corps within"—Andre 98. The attack involved six companies of British Regulars.

21   "in the warmest terms"—Hatch 77, quoting Andre to his sister in England. Referring to his commander, General Grey, and the Paoli butch-
ery, Andre says that Grey "is much respected in the army, and this last
coup has gained him much credit." Hatch comments justly: "Andre
seems to have had no qualms about his part in the slaughter."

22   *The dragoon cloak*: Sparks 258-59. In a letter Tallmadge recalls that
while on the way to Tappan from West Point, Andre repeatedly complained of his nondescript apparel, to the point where he felt moved
to do something about it: "Andre kept reviewing his shabby dress, and
finally remarked to me that he was positively ashamed to go to the
headquarters of the American army in such a plight. I called my servant
and directed him to bring my dragoon cloak, which I presented to
Major Andre. This he refused to take for some time; but I insisted on
it, and he finally put it on and rode in it to Tappan."

Perhaps it really was as innocent as that, a simple matter of personal
or say military vanity. Yet since Andre's civilian clothing would become
a crucial part of the charge against him, his wanting to hide the evidence when first appearing among his judges does take on some coloring
of deliberate calculation. As was later established, when he came ashore
for the meeting with Arnold he had a heavy civilian overcoat covering

his uniform. On changing to civilian dress he evidently discarded the overcoat, which itself became an item of significance in the effort to judge his true status. The nankeen pants he wore *were* part of his uniform. But civilians also wore such, as did the officers of many armies then. The distinctive part of the uniform was the scarlet, swallowtailed, gold-epauletted tunic. In place of his military tricorn hat, Andre when captured had on a derby-like fedora with a circular brim.

II: IN THE COURTROOM

23 *Trial sources*: The official record of the Andre inquiry is that compiled for and approved by Washington, and published as a pamphlet by Congress in October 1780, three weeks after the trial (see the bibliography under *Proceedings*). No detailed account of the questioning is supplied, nor is a sequential record given of the various points covered, only in general. However, a good deal of latent information is embedded in the text of the *Proceedings*, much of it extractable under close analysis. In this way, and drawing on discussions of the trial by serious students (Hamilton, J. H. Smith, Mahon, Biddle, Haines, Sargent, Flexner, Hatch, Koke, etc.), it has been possible to recover at least the essential steps and topics of the one-day inquiry.

In assigning interrogatories to the various judges I have tried to fit question to questioner according to known interests and backgrounds. The questions themselves are either known or are those that *must* have been asked. The answers are either known or reflect those that Andre *must* have replied in light of the documented circumstances.

23 *Washington's instructions to the court*: Proceedings 8-9.
25 *Andre's letter to Washington*: Proceedings 9-13.
29 "the hellish plot"—Greene 315.
31 *The treason documents*: The originals are preserved in the New York State Library at Albany. The complete contents have been variously published: see for instance Abbatt 16-18. Only one word is adequate to describe Andre's retaining these papers on his person after learning that his return would not be directly to the ship but overland—stupidity. More than one perplexed commentator has asked why he didn't simply reduce all the essential information in them in code to a single sheet of paper, unreadable by anyone else. He could easily have done it in an hour before leaving the Smith house. His own commander,

General Clinton, said that the papers were not essential and should have been discarded.

33 *Andre's statement to the court*: The original of this has not survived but the entire text is printed from manuscript in Sargent 392-94. In the *Proceedings* it appears in paraphrase (13-14), which also includes some of Andre's replies to questions prompted by the statement.

36 *The captors located*: After delivering their prisoner to the American military authorities at North Castle the three captors returned to their militia units, neglecting to put their identities or addresses on record. When Washington ordered them sent to his headquarters at West Point, only one, John Paulding, could be immediately located. On September 27 he was sent to Washington carrying a message from Colonel Jameson who commanded at North Castle: "This note will be delivered to you by John Paulding, one of the young men that took Major Andre, and who nobly refused any sum of money that could be offered. The other two young men that were in company with him are not yet found. As soon as they arrive they shall be sent on" (Raymond 4, no source cited).

The second man, David Williams, must have turned up soon after, for he testified at the trial of Joshua Smith in Tappan a few days later. The third man, Isaac Van Wart, did not testify at the Smith trial, so must not have been located for another week or so. The comment of Marcus Raymond is apt: "So they were not running around, as some would have us believe, with their hats in their hands" begging for a reward. "Like modest, self-respecting men, having done their duty [they] went their several ways, and had to be sent for that they might be taken into the presence of the Commander-in-Chief" (Raymond 4). The three did receive prize money equivalent to Andre's horse, saddle, and gold watch, as well as the pension voted them by Congress.

41 *The error as to neutral territory*: This exchange regarding the point of capture does not appear in the *Proceedings*, which indeed makes no mention of the error (nor has it been noticed by any other writer since then). But it is glaring when realized, and I think *must* have arisen at the trial.

42 *Firing on the* Vulture: See above, 84-85, and below, 202.

43 "Major Andre . . . is assuredly"—Van Doren 486.

45 *Andre at the plot's center*: For the secret correspondence between Andre and Arnold during 1779-80 see Van Doren 441-75. Arnold made the

initial approach to the English, but Clinton soon put Andre in charge
of the delicate negotiations.

45 *Andre's final statement: Proceedings* 18.

48 "The Board having considered"—*Proceedings* 24-26. Note the emphasis
on the secret nature of the meeting with Arnold, under cover
of night, and on the fact that Andre by his own admission had
been within American lines in disguise and with a bogus identity. But
the error about the point of capture being "within our lines" is not
repeated.

III: ANDRE FOR ARNOLD?

50 *Washington's decision on Arnold:* Van Doren 392-94; Freeman 217-20;
79; Irving 152-54; Koke 111-12. That Washington was terribly shaken
by Arnold's defection is a fact allowed by all his biographers, and is
hardly surprising. It is also a fact that he recovered promptly and began
plotting the traitor's punishment. His feelings in the matter are well
summed up by Bakeless: "The personal bitterness of General Washington toward the traitor Arnold was without parallel in the life of that
magnanimous man. Though the commander-in-chief had to approve
many death sentences, Arnold was the only man he ever really *wanted*
to hang" (302).

Some commentators, more punctilious and citing the day's code of
military honor, decry Washington's mere attempt to work an exchange
of Andre for Arnold. It was beneath his dignity, they charge in all
seriousness. The truth is that all sides were quite ready to work a deal
behind the scenes if it were at all possible—more so because there was
some thought that the sneaking Arnold had arranged matters so that
in case of discovery Andre would be sacrificed while he escaped. Why
Clinton, no stranger to clandestine expediency, failed to join in is a
separate question.

51 "Major Andre was taken"—Fitzpatrick 103.

52 *Andre's letter to General Clinton: Proceedings* 27-29. The letter is dated
September 29, and was written shortly after Andre was dismissed
from the courtroom, while he was waiting to hear the court's decision. But at this moment he was fairly confident of being acquitted of
the charge of spying and being sent instead to a prison camp, from
where he expected he would eventually be exchanged. His remark

about "the rigorous determination that is impending" certainly did not refer to a possible death sentence. As I suggest, the body of the letter was perfectly calculated to reinforce the claims he had presented at the trial and was intended as much for Washington's eyes as for Clinton's.

53 *Captain Ogden's mission*: Ogden 23-25; Lossing 768-69; Sparks 267-70; Sargent 410-12; Van Doren 363-67. Some details of the mission differ slightly from source to source concerning how and when Ogden did what he did. They're not hard to reconcile, however.

54 "The Commander in Chief"—Fitzpatrick XX, 104.

55 "If Sir Henry will"—Sargent 411. Sargent says the message was given to Ogden by General LaFayette, but the evidence favors it coming directly from Washington. That it was written down for Ogden to memorize is my own conclusion. Of course the phrase "in any way" is the key, and any number of "ways" can be imagined, including one in which Clinton simply gave his word of honor to deliver Arnold in some manner later, bringing Andre's instant release in a token exchange of prisoners.

In the packet of letters delivered to Clinton by Ogden, it seems that there was a note written in a disguised hand pointing out the "double treachery" planned by Arnold which called for sacrificing Andre to his own safety if needed. Whether the assertion was literally true no one knows. In any case the note misfired (Hendrickson 287-88; Van Doren 366-67).

55 "I am persuaded the"—Van Doren 488.

56 *Stay of execution*: Sargent 417-18.

57 *Conference of Greene and Robertson*: Van Doren 488-92; Greene 236-39; Sargent 427-30; Freeman 218-20. The suggestion that both Washington and Greene understood this riverside conference as Clinton's encouraging response to Washington's veiled offer of an exchange is my own. The evidence strongly points that way, and I find it surprising that the suggestion hasn't been made before this. The reason, I think, is the reluctance of historians to show Washington engaged in such unmilitary hugger-mugger.

57 "The case of an acknowledged"—Van Doren 488. This is the written report of General Robertson to Clinton, the main source for what happened at the conference. The quotations in the following paragraphs are from this same report. Later that same day Robertson wrote and

sent by messenger a letter directly to Washington recapping the meeting with Greene. It arrived too late, but of course would have made no difference.

59   *Arnold's threatening letter*: Van Doren 490, where it is quoted whole. Why Arnold would have thought that such a bare-faced threat would have any effect on Washington, why Clinton deigned to send the letter, are puzzles, perhaps to be explained only by the critical urgency of the situation.

59   "I flatter myself I"—Sargent 397.

60   *Honora Sneyd*: The true facts of Andre's relationship with this young woman are now well understood. No doubt Andre did feel some leftover affection for Honora after losing her to another man. But he was soon busy in America paying attention to Yankee belles, including Peggy Chew, daughter of a prominent Philadelphia family. The high point of the romantic legend in the nineteenth century was reached with an article in the *Atlantic Monthly*, "John Andre and Honora Sneyd" (December 1860), by Winthrop Sargent. The 1861 biography of Andre by Sargent gives it even lengthier treatment. See also Tillotson 18-27; Flexner 21-29; and Hatch 18-24, 277.

61   "his flesh seeming to"—Garden 291.

61   "truly suffered in"—Idzerda 182.

61   "He was a charming man"—Idzerda 195. The letter was written five days after Andre's execution. The reference to Andre is only a small part of the letter's contents.

62   "military glory, the"—Sparks 257.

62   "that I can remember no"—Tallmadge 57.

62   "as cheerful as if he"—Tallmadge 133.

62   *Andre sketching*: The night scene of the Hudson River shore has often been reproduced, first in New York City in 1780 as a broadside with the explanation that Andre's friend, Lieutenant Colonel Crosbie, "has caused this engraving to be made from the original in his possession as a small mark of his friendship for that very valuable and unfortunate officer." A copy of the engraving is in the Lenox Library, New York City (the original drawing is lost). The self-portrait of the seated Andre was not done, as some say, on the morning of his execution. It was done on the previous evening before he learned of the failed Greene-Robertson negotiations, and while he still expected to be saved. The original is at Yale University. For Ensign Tomlinson's reaction to An-

dre's apparent facility see Sparks 280. Some half-dozen of Andre's self-portaits still survive.

IV: THE DAYS BEFORE — BLUNDER

68   *The Andre-Arnold negotiations:* The complete secret correspondence is given in Van Doren 439-81. It began in May 1779, so was in progress for sixteen months before their meeting on the Hudson shore.

69   *Andre departs the* Vulture: J. H. Smith 28-30; Koke 83-84, Dawson 10-15, 74-76. The overcoat was supplied by Captain Sutherland of the *Vulture:* see Sutherland's letter to Clinton in Van Doren 493-94. At first, it seems, Andre declined the coat, saying he had been ordered "to go in his uniform." What made him change his mind is not stated, but part of the reason must have been the need to conceal his identity from the Cahoon brothers, and ostensibly from Smith. Probably there was also some fear of an accidental sighting, despite the darkness.

70   "Mr. Anderson, from his"—Smith, J. H., 31.

70   *The brothers Cahoon:* Dawson 5-17; Koke 141-43; J. H. Smith 25-27, 136-38. The name was spelled *Colquhoun,* pronounced *Cuh-hoon,* leading to the simplified form.

71   *The trip to shore and the meeting with Arnold:* J. H. Smith 30-32; Van Doren 331-34; Sargent 323-25; Pennypacker 144-151; Koke 84-86; Dawson 6-8. Wilson's 1885 article identifying Andre's landing place at Long Clove Mountain mentions "traces of an old dock and of an ancient road made for the purpose of reaching it . . . the most reliable tradition fixes this old dock as the landing-place of Andre" (175). He admits, however, that the dock may have been "rebuilt and enlarged after the Revolution" (176). Wilson also makes a good point, one generally overlooked, about the landing place. It had to be specifically agreed on beforehand, and had to center on some readily identifiable feature, "so definite that no time might be lost, and no shouting or signals needed which might betray them . . . Yet the normal features of the shore in this vicinity for the distance of a mile are so uniform that it would have been extremely difficult to designate any spot unless marked, as this one was, by improvements from human hands." The fact that there was a small dock at Long Clove was probably known to Smith, a long-time resident of the area. A second article on the landing

place by Wilson written twenty-five years later (1910) reports that the dock was still there: "it is much decayed, but some of the timbers still remain buried in the stones, and a small portion of its south wall is still standing" (333). Today nothing remains.

The conversation between Arnold and Andre at their meeting is nowhere specifically described, neither man leaving anything on record beyond Andre's few comments. But there is a good deal of collateral evidence, and the points mentioned in my text would necessarily have been covered by the two plotters. See Sargent 327-31; Randall 545-46; Flexner 346-48; Van Doren 332-33; and various portions of the articles by Haines, Biddle, and Willcox.

72   *The treason papers*: Previously it has been assumed that these were given to Andre by Arnold at the Smith house. That is clearly wrong. Obviously they had been prepared well before the night of the meeting, and since Andre expected to return promptly that same night directly to the ship, the papers would have been given to him initially at the meeting on the shore. This is supported by Andre's later explanation that "when I went into the boat I should have them [the papers] tied about with a string and a stone" (Andre's statement to the court, quoted in Sargent 393). The stone was a precaution, allowing him to get rid of the papers quickly, completely, and finally, if need be, by dropping them into the river.

Relevant in this regard also is a comment offered by Sparks in his biography of Arnold: "Since Arnold himself went down to meet Andre at the Clove, it may be inferred that he thought everything might possibly be completed there; otherwise he would have been more likely to wait for him at Smith's house" (204). This also bears on the question of whether Andre fully expected and intended to return directly to the ship from his secret shoreside meeting. That was obviously the plan of both Andre and Arnold.

Andre's later claim that he accepted the papers only because Arnold "insisted" is of a piece with his overall defensive posture that *everything* he did while ashore was the result of someone's "insisting," either Arnold's or Smith's. It is marvelous how he expected that this would excuse his actions, or even that he would be believed.

73   *Payment to Arnold*: Two weeks after Andre's death, Arnold raised anew with Clinton the question of the compensation his treason should bring, restating his original demand of twenty thousand pounds for suc-

cess, half that in any case. He said that Andre at their meeting had led him to believe that those figures were acceptable to Clinton. What he got was six thousand pounds plus expenses, also life pensions for his wife and children. He also received pay and emoluments of a brevet brigadier general, with retirement rank of a lieutenant-colonel of horse (Randall 575; Van Doren 384-88).

73 "commissioned to promise"—Van Doren 480-81, which quotes Arnold's haggling letter to Clinton of October 18 reporting his talk with Andre on the matter of payment. Not at all backward about pressing his case, Arnold adds regarding his demand for the ten thousand rather than the six: "I beg leave to observe that it is far short of the loss I have sustained . . . I am induced with the greatest cheerfulness to submit the matter to Your Excellency, in full confidence of your generous intentions, and that you will not think my claim unreasonable when you consider the sacrifices I have made, and that the sum is a trifling object to the Public tho of consequence to me."

74 *The Hudson River tides*: The role played by the river itself in this part of the treason drama went wholly unnoticed until Smith gave it a passing mention in his 1808 *Narrative*. The Cahoon brothers, he said, asked by Arnold to row Andre back to the ship, "declared themselves unable to gratify his wish, through want of strength to accomplish it, and the ebb tide being against them" (32; for *ebb* read *flood*). Sargent in 1861 mentioned the tide when telling how the rowboat went to the *Vulture* to bring Andre off, but overlooked it when explaining the failure to return him to the ship that night. Except for a brief, inconclusive discussion in 1899 by Abbatt (6), no other writer has bothered with the question of the tides (Koke 86 quotes Smith and lets it go at that). But it clearly and certainly was the adverse tide that determined the Cahoons' refusal. Having myself canoed and rowboated on the Hudson when young, I can add my personal witness to that judgment.

75 "he was afraid to go"—Dawson 8, quoting Cahoon's testimony at the Smith trial. This was said to Smith in Arnold's presence, upon which Arnold sternly charged, "if I was a friend to my country I should do my best . . . Upon my saying what was the reason he could not stay [wait] till morning, General Arnold said it must be done that night . . . said if I did not go he would look upon me as a disaffected man."

75 "I asked him why the"—Dawson 12, also from testimony at the Smith

trial. A more convenient source for the Cahoons' testimony is Van Doren 327-29.

75 "too late to fetch me"—Andre's trial statement quoted in Sargent 393. No one involved that night would have had the least idea that the meeting might last until it was "too late" to get Andre back to the ship. The whole point of meeting in that fashion and at that place was to conclude the business expeditiously and promptly return the British agent to safety.

76 "Measures might have been"—Van Doren 493 quotes Sutherland's original letter whole. Curiously, no other writer on the Andre affair notices this assertion of the ship's captain, but it makes a significant point about Andre's failure to do anything like adequate planning for his mission. Notice Sutherland's emphatic phrase, "he very well knew," which makes the captain's anguish and embarrassment quite plain.

77 "passed a guard I did"—Andre's trial statement, Sargent 393.

77 "upon ground not within"—*Proceedings* 10-11. Andre's deft phrasing in this letter and his use of such waffling terms as "conducted" manage to cloud the contradiction, glaring as it is. He says that he met Arnold on neutral ground and *stipulated* to him that he must not be taken within American lines. But Arnold ignored the stipulation, he says, and "without my knowledge beforehand" escorted him into the enemy camp. But since they encountered a sentry on the way in, Andre *did* have knowledge beforehand of his destination, and could have turned back. The most arresting instance of Andre's particular brand of *chutzpah* in the whole affair is his coolly stating in his letter that once inside American lines he had "become a prisoner" and of necessity had to "concert my escape." Writing those words he must have smiled at his own audacity.

79 *The firing on the Vulture*: Smith 33, 36; Abbatt 12-13; Van Doren 334-35, 474; Dawson 15-16, 76; Rawson 48, Leake 258.

80 ". . . on Thursday night"—Van Doren 475, which gives Robinson's letter, a long one reporting to Clinton on the events of the several days previous.

81 ". . . at 5 the rebels"—Sargent 328 quotes from the original log, now in the Public Record Office, London. A copy is in the Rockland County (New York) Historical Society.

81 "at half past five"—Sargent 329, quoting from the original.

82 "Vulture off Sinsink"—Van Doren 474. Robinson explains that the

ship's captain has sent for a support vessel, "if it should be necessary for us to continue here any time longer." Next day the ship came back upriver a mile or so, but on the 25th it dropped all the way back down to New York City, anchoring off the present Spuyten Duyvil at Manhattan's northern tip.

V: THE DAYS BEFORE — FLIGHT

83 *Andre at the Smith house*: J. H. Smith 34-37; Dawson 15, 62-63, 75; Campbell 24-26; Sargent 337; Abbatt 10-14; Randall 547; Flexner 349-52; Koke 87-92. Known locally as "Treason House," it was visited by Lossing about 1850, who found it well cared for, the property of a William Houseman "whose good taste has adorned the grounds around it with fine shrubbery" (750). From the window in a second-story bedroom through which Andre gazed longingly at the *Vulture*, Lossing made a pencil sketch of the scene down to the river, still looking very much as it had appeared to Andre (see p. 78). For a while there was some idea of preserving the house, but it gradually fell into disrepair and in 1980 was pulled down. A hospital now occupies the site.

84 *The Vulture incident*: There is confusion as to just when that morning the firing on the ship occurred, whether just as Arnold and Andre reached the house or somewhat later. I think the evidence places it a bit later, about as I show it. Of course neither Andre nor Arnold left any description of what they saw out that window or what was said between them. But again the available evidence yields sufficiently definite information to allow a reliable reconstruction: for the sources used see the previous note.

86 *Andre's change to civilian clothes*: At the trial the fact of Andre's being in disguise was covered by the Board in a series of questions put to the prisoner. In his letter to Washington Andre had confessed to being "an enemy in disguise within your posts" (*Proceedings* 11). Washington in his instructions to the court had specified this charge, referring to "a disguised habit" (*Proceedings* 8). The questioning by the Board is summed up in the *Proceedings* in a single sentence: Andre was inside American lines "in the dress he is at present in, and which he said was not his regimentals, and which dress he procured after he landed from the *Vulture*, when he was within our post" (14). The Board's verdict specified that Andre's change of dress did in fact take place within

American lines, and that when he passed the guard-posts during his escape attempt he was "in a disguised habit" (*Proceedings* 25).

This charge in itself, it seems, was enough to classify Andre as a spy and make him liable to hanging. The incriminating papers found on him of course sealed off any possible alternate conclusion. It should also be noted that in the discussion between the British and the Americans over Andre's status, the British *never* refer to the question of his having been in disguise.

The only eyewitness description of how and when the change of clothing was made occurs in Smith's 1808 *Narrative*. First he implies that when meeting Andre initially aboard the *Vulture* he noticed only "boots, and a large blue great-coat" (29), all sign of a uniform being hidden under the coat. But at his own trial in 1780 Smith had admitted that the overcoat was open at the breast revealing "a red coat" underneath which he was unable to tell was a uniform or simply a red civilian jacket (Dawson 28; but of course the distinctive scarlet of the British uniform was never used in civilian clothing). Later at his house, Smith explained, Arnold informed him that "Anderson had come on shore in a military dress, which he had borrowed, from pride or vanity, from an officer of his acquaintance at New York; that as it would be impossible for him to travel in that uniform he requested the loan of one of my coats. Being nearly of my size, I lent him a coat: the other part of his dress, he said, did not require change" (*Narrative* 36).

The epauletted tunic was carefully folded and laid away in a bureau drawer in one of the bedrooms. After Andre's capture when the house was searched, the tunic was found and became part of the evidence against both Andre and Smith (Koke 141).

86 *Arrival of Smith at the house:* J. H. Smith 34; Dawson 15-16; Koke 87.

87 *The three passes:* Van Doren 335-36; Koke 89-91, where two of the passes are given in facsimile; Sargent 393 (Andre's statement to the court).

88 "From this time he"—J. H. Smith 37.

89 "and with a heavy sigh"—J. H. Smith 36.

89 *Clinton's three orders to Andre: Proceedings* 28 (in Andre's own letter); Van Doren 329, quoting a letter of Clinton's; Sargent 393.

89 "thus become a prisoner"—*Proceedings* 11.

90 ". . . the events of coming"—*Proceedings* 28.

90 "I have ommitted mentioning"—Sargent 394 (Andre's statement to the court).

91 "objected much against"—Sargent 393 (Andre's statement to the court), same for the next quotation in this paragraph.

91 *The escape route*: J. H. Smith 37-47; Abbatt 14-15, 19-25; Koke 93-98; Dawson 34-42, 49-52; Campbell 26 (the ferryman's testimony).

92 *Stopped by Captain Boyd*: Pennypacker 155-57, quoting the statement of Boyd himself supplied for the Smith trial; Koke 95-96; Dawson 42-47; J. H. Smith 39-41 (Captain Bull here is an error for Boyd).

93 "On approaching the house"—J. H. Smith 40.

94 "and my companion"—J. H. Smith 41.

95 "We slept in the same"—J. H. Smith 43.

96 *The encounter with Colonel Webb*: Webb 296, quoting a letter of Lieutenant Joshua King to whom Andre told the story; Koke 97, 270; Abbatt 22.

96 "he thought himself"—J. H. Smith 42.

96 ". . . his countenance brightened"—J. H. Smith 44.

97 "made a good meal"—J. H. Smith 47.

97 *Parting of Andre and Smith*: J. H. Smith 47-48; Koke 98-99; Sargent 344. Why Smith allowed Andre to go on alone has never been adequately explained. Abbatt 23 states well the puzzlement felt by many: "At this stage of the journey Smith and he parted—to his speedy ruin. Nothing has ever been disclosed as to why this was done . . . Andre knew nothing of the region between, while Smith knew it well. He had agreed to take his companion there [to New York] but made no further effort to that end. The other could not force him to do it, and possibly did not greatly desire his further company, feeling tolerably confident, as Smith told him he was now beyond the American outposts." Sargent (344) thought that Smith was simply afraid of encountering trouble in the lawless Neutral Ground, and Smith's biographer, Richard Koke, agrees: "The increasing danger of the Neutral Ground was making Smith wary, and . . . he informed Anderson he would accompany him no further" (98). But that's hardly the whole story, and I think a good part of the reason was Smith's not knowing the full extent of the conspiracy or Andre's role in it. If Smith was part of the plot he would surely have escorted Andre all the way to safety in New York. His not doing so was of a piece with his failure to return Andre directly to the *Vulture* from the riverside meeting with Arnold. He simply didn't understand the

urgency, and in any case was eager to avoid the remaining fifteen miles of horseback riding, as well as being less than eager to face the uncertainties of an encounter with the Cowboys or Skinners. Even so, I'll admit that the question of why he abandoned Andre at Pine's Bridge is still an open one.

VI: THE DAYS BEFORE — CAPTURE

99 *John Paulding*: For his background see the articles by Drimmer, Brown, and Roe; also Constant 171-74; Abbatt 28-29; Benson 131-32; and various records in the archives of the Field Library, Peekskill, New York. For his prison escape see *Centennial* 162-63, and Meade 274, 277 (description by an old comrade who shared his captivity).

100 "furnished him with"—*Centennial* 162.

101 "continually patrolling"—Roe 5, see also Drimmer 51.

102 *Williams and Van Wart*: For personal background see the articles by Drimmer, Sullivan, Brown, and Roe; and Benson 143-34. Also for Williams, Roscoe 135-37, 464-65, and Raymond 5-7. According to Williams the two men were first cousins.

103 *Testimony of the captors*: Separate descriptions of Andre's capture were left by each of the captors, the two basic ones, by Paulding and Williams, coming in the form of sworn testimony at the trial of Joshua Smith. At different times over the years all three provided further statements, adding to the picture, if also slightly confusing it. Though all the accounts are unstudied—rambling recitals without benefit of professional guidance—taken together they afford enough detail to permit a reliable reconstruction of the famous and fateful incident.

No single source gives all the statements, and there is much repetition. I use a total of eleven: Sparks 223-26; Dawson *passim*; Simms 646-52; Pennypacker 161-64; *Historical Magazine* I, 293-95, VIII, 366-68 (1857); Benson 13-21; Roscoe 136-37; *The Schoharie Union*, 29 September 1876; Raymond 6-9; *Centennial* 61-65, 144.

103 "simple peasants, leaning"—Hamilton 22. Some writers incorrectly assign these words to other Hamilton letters.

103 "A beautiful region of"—Irving 109.

104 *Jesse Thorn*: Abbatt 24.

106 *Washington as target*: Hamilton 12-13; Sargent 332; Van Doren 362; Washington himself doubted that he'd been a prime target of the plot.

He felt it would have been a mistake for the British to complicate their main objective, the taking of West Point, by concentrating to any extent on him.

106   *Sally Hammond*: Abbatt 25.

107   *The capture*: The picture I give of this crucial event rests on close study of the three captors' various statements, listed just above. I have *not* drawn on the several versions that trace back to Andre himself (King, Bronson, Tallmadge, etc.) for reasons made clear at this chapter's close and in chapter 9. The greater part of the dialogue is exactly what was recorded by the captors, at times expanded a bit, or it closely paraphrases their actual language in describing the scene. No more than a quarter of the dialogue, all of it incidental, is reconstructed, but this too I have placed in quotes. Giving this small portion without quotes while using them for the rest produces a choppy effect all too liable to confuse.

112   "a ludicrous sketch"—Irving 116; see also Sparks 235.

113   ". . . damn Arnold's pass"—Webb 296, quoting King's letter.

113   "They seized him, robbed"—Sargent 358, quoting Bowman.

113   "unbosomed his heart"—Hall 62, quoting Tallmadge's letter.

114   ". . . only because they"—Sargent 521, quoting Tallmadge in 1817. see above, 160-69, and below, 217-18.

VII: THE DAYS BEFORE — EXPOSURE

115   *Colonel Jameson's blunder*: Sparks 227-30; Abbatt 35-37; Van Doren 340-42. In a contrite note to Washington (Abbatt 52; Van Doren 342) Jameson apologized for his blunder. Washington forgave him but only after a withering comment on his "egregious folly, or bewildered conception" in which he "seemed lost in astonishment, and not to know what he was doing" (Sparks 230). Attempts have been made to defend Jameson's action as militarily correct (Sargent 362; Abbatt 36), but in the end the decision goes against him. What he *should* have done in that unprecedented situation, particularly after hearing Tallmadge's arguments, is obvious. Holding both Andre and the papers in custody at North Castle, he should have dispatched by express rider to Washington a note of explanation—or two notes in two directions to make certain of reaching him—and waited for instructions. The fact that after allowing himself to be persuaded by Tallmadge to recall Andre he *still*

insisted on sending a note to Arnold shows his unfortunate lack of grasp and failure of nerve in dealing with a superior.

116   "I have sent Lieutenant Allen"—Van Doren 485-86. If *both* Andre and the damning papers had reached Arnold, the plot *still* might have succeeded. Andre could have gone promptly back to the city by way of the *Vulture*, setting off the British attack upriver.

117   *Tallmadge's late return*: Tallmadge 51-52. He says that he'd been on patrol with his troop all day and returned to North Castle "late in the evening of the 23rd," when he was told "that a prisoner had been brought in that day by the name of John Anderson," then quickly "learned the circumstances of the capture of the prisoner."

117   *Prior knowledge of "Anderson"*—*Proceedings* 16-17; Flexner 329-30; Sargent 292-93.

118   "I was very much"—Tallmadge 52.

120   "I have had many"—Tallmadge 136.

120   "the proposals which were"—Tallmadge 137.

121   *Jameson's note to Arnold*: Van Doren 486. Note that Jameson directs Allen to take Andre to lower (South) Salem, not back to North Castle. Tallmadge's later memory tricked him on this detail, for in his *Memoir* (53-53) he has Andre being returned to North Castle, then next day being transferred to South Salem.

122   "bloody with spurring"—Garden 293.

123   "He looked somewhat"—Webb 295-96 (the printing of King's letter in *Mag. of History*, 1889 gives only a portion of it, and dates it June 17, 1817, instead of July 17). Same for the quotations from King in the following paragraphs.

123   "as soon as I saw"—Tallmadge 53. Same for the quotation in the next paragraph.

124   "When I received and"—Tallmadge 53-54. Probably Tallmadge was right in calculating that Arnold would have had warning long before he could reach West Point with a troop of cavalry. Only on reading Andre's confession in the letter to Washington could Tallmadge have been sure enough of his ground to go after Arnold. By then some ten or twelve hours had passed since Lieutenant Allen left South Salem carrying Jameson's note to Arnold. Still it's a pity that he didn't, even at that late hour, make the attempt, since as it turned out Allen was rather delayed in reaching Arnold.

124   ". . . they had ripped up"—Dykman, 54.

125 *Andre's letter to Washington: Proceedings* 9-13. With Andre's studied phrasing it is easy to miss the letter's flagrant contradictions, centering on his wish to avoid being thought of as having "a mean character." He says that he writes *not* out of fear or concern "for my safety," *not* in order to "solicit security," only to protect his standing as a gentleman. Yet at the letter's end he makes his personal safety a main issue, threatening physical harm to any number of American prisoners if physical harm touches him—and threatening not too subtly. The Americans being held at Charleston, he writes, "are persons whom the treatment I receive might affect."

Then take his opening words about having lied to his captors in concealing his identity, his business, and his movements. Those lies, he claims, were quite "justifiable" in his effort to escape. Of course they were. Would any man of sense think that lying in such a situation needed explanation? He adds that his lies failed because he is "too little accustomed to duplicity." Does he seriously believe that if he'd been a better liar he could have explained away his possession of those incriminating papers? No, he is simply *ignoring* that aspect of his situation, another of his tactics. Writing such a letter at all in those circumstances surely was in itself not only "dishonorable" but eminently self-serving, not to say thickheaded.

The British, recognizing that Andre's letter was in fact a clear confession of guilt, tried to dismiss it as unreliable, penned at a time when Andre was in a "low-spirited" condition, unfit to speak sensibly. He stated facts reasonably enough, but "reasoned ill upon them" (General Robertson's report to Clinton after his meeting with Greene, Van Doren 489). It was because of this confessional letter and the statement in court that no witnesses were called at the trial and that the trial lasted only a day.

128 *Escape of Benedict Arnold: Proceedings* 3-4; Hamilton 12; Randall 552, 555; Flexner 366-68. The interval between Arnold's rushed escape and Washington's arrival, according to Hamilton, was about an hour, but it actually might have been less than half that. In discussing this dramatic near-miss commentators imply that if Washington had arrived earlier Arnold would have been caught. That is unlikely. The note from Jameson that tipped Arnold arrived in the morning, the papers that alerted Washington came in the afternoon. Even if Arnold was in Washington's presence when handed Jameson's note, he could have

dissembled long enough to make his exit from the room, then making a dash for the river, as he actually did.

The apparent delay in Lieutenant Allen's arrival at Arnold's headquarters has not before been noticed. He certainly did deposit Andre at South Salem early on the morning of September 24. He didn't reach Arnold's headquarters until the morning of the 25th, between seven and eight o'clock. The ride from South Salem to West Point would have taken at most six hours. When exactly Lieutenant Allen departed South Salem, what speed he made, and whether he stopped along the way have never been established. I show him leaving South Salem on the morning of September 24, which is a reasonable deduction from the circumstances. But of course that would have put him at West Point by at most late afternoon of the 24th. Yet he didn't show up until early morning of the 25th. If he didn't leave South Salem until late on the 24th, what could have kept him there? He was, after all, under orders to deliver Jameson's letter to West Point, "and return as soon as you can do your business" (Van Doren 486). Even if he stopped long enough for some sleep, at South Salem or along the way, he should still have reached West Point sometime the night of the 24th.

129 "as Washington made the"—Freeman 198. Same for the quotations in the next paragraph.

130 "Whom can we trust"—Sargent 375.

130 *Washington's reaction: Proceedings* 5; Freeman 199-205; Abbatt 43-45; Irving 122-25.

131 "was forced open with"—J. H. Smith 49-50. Same for the quotations in the next paragraph.

132 "Major Andre cannot be"—Sparks 250-51

134 *Transfer of Andre to West Point*: Hatch 250-51; Abbatt 48-50.

134 "The rain fell in"—Hatch 251.

VIII: FAREWELL PERFORMANCE

138 *Andre's letter to Washington: Proceedings* 42-43; Hamilton 16-17, same for Washington's silence, meant to spare Andre "the sensations which a certain knowledge of the intended mode would inflict." Washington simply could not grant the request of a spy for death by a firing squad rather than the gallows. The only reason advanced by anyone for doing so was Andre's personal feelings of "honor," his position as a gentleman-

officer. But such privilege of class, its effects at least, was among the very reasons why the colonies had rebelled in the first place. That fact, curiously, is forgotten even today by overly sensitive commentators.

In any case, Andre's short note soon took its place among the nineteenth century's admired literature. Sixty years after it was written, N. P. Willis turned it into verse, the little poem itself gaining a measure of fame:

> *It is not the fear of death*
> *that damps my brow;*
> *It is not for another breath*
> *I ask thee now.*
> *I can die with a lip unstirred*
> *And a quiet heart—*
> *Let but this prayer be heard*
> *Ere I depart.*
>
> *I can give up my mother's look,*
> *My sister's kiss;*
> *I can think of love, yet brook*
> *A death like this!*
> *I can forget the lasting fame*
> *I burn'd to win,*
> *All—but the spotless name*
> *I glory in! etc.*

138 *Andre executed in uniform*: It is strange how the fact of Andre's wearing his scarlet regimental tunic to his hanging is invariably noted by every historian, yet none ever asks how or why it happened. A spy captured in civilian disguise naturally would not be permitted to appear on the gallows in military regalia. Yet Andre, while being executed as a spy, was allowed that privilege. No record or explanation of the move survives, not even in the form of a question. Yet it is quite certain that only Washington could have given the order that permitted the indulgence. He was not always the unbending legalist.

It is said that the uniform Andre wore on the gallows was a replacement brought up from New York City by Andre's servant. That may be, but I incline to think it was really the same jacket that Andre doffed at Smith's house and which was laid away in a bureau drawer. That jacket was quickly found on a search of the house within hours of Andre's capture, and there is no record of what became of it later, if not worn by Andre at his execution.

139   "leave me until you"—Sargent 417. Here again, Andre's harsh dismissal of his grieving servant has been praised as demonstrating the admirable grip he had on his emotions that final morning. Of course it does nothing of the sort. What had the tears of a dedicated servant to do with Andre's personal behavior? Ordering the servant out of his sight until he could appear "more manly" shows only how carefully Andre wished to stage-manage his exit.

140   "Gentlemen, I'm ready"—Thatcher 227; Sargent 441. The actual words quoted are, "I am ready, gentlemen, at any moment to wait on you." But the phrase *to wait on you* really means *to receive you*, and the two guards were already in the room, and it was to them that he spoke. In my view *proceed* is what he said, or something very like it.

141   "I am much surprised"—Abbatt 71. As with many staple details of the Andre story, this remark is always allowed to pass without comment. But its entire fatuousness is evident. What had "discipline" to do with troops lined up for an execution? If Andre really meant "well-drilled," the comment was even less fitting, and the same in even stronger degree goes for his remark on the "music." As a whole, the observation at *such* a time could have come only from a supercilious mind. In my view, Andre here came perilously close to inadvertent self-parody.

142   "Such fortitude I"—Flexner 391, quoting Hart's letter.

142   "between two of our"—Thatcher 227.

142   *The march to the gallows*: Hamilton 17; Thatcher 227-28; Abbatt 71-73; Tallmadge 56; Sargent 442-43. Several times I have made the long walk from Andre's prison in the Mabie Tavern up the hill to the gallows site, keeping to a measured pace while imagining that I could hear the repeated mournful rolling of the drums and the muted fifes. My conclusion is that Andre's last walk occupied twelve, perhaps fifteen minutes, most of it on a rising grade.

143   "What's the matter?"—Thatcher 228. What the diarist, an eyewitness of the scene, actually has Bowman asking Andre when he recoiled at the sight of the gallows is, "Why this emotion, sir?" Andre's reply he gives as, "I am reconciled to my death, but I detest the mode" (compare

Hamilton 17). I believe that in both instances (and in others I have let stand) the phrasing has been silently improved to fit the day's taste in such things. Would any man of intelligence ask a prisoner in the shadow of the gibbet, "Why this emotion?" I give the phrases as they probably sounded. See also Tallmadge 56, where Andre, when told he must die by hanging, is quoted as saying, "How hard is my Fate!" With good reason, I feel, in my text I have changed this to something less theatrical.

144   *Tallmadge's farewell to Andre*: Webb 294, quoting a letter of Tallmadge to Colonel Wadsworth, October 4, 1780, two days after the execution. "He met death with a smile," wrote Tallmadge, "cheerfully marching to the place of execution, and bidding his friends, those who had been with him, farewell. He called me to him a few minutes before he swung off, and expressed his gratitude to me for my civilities in such a way, and so cheerfully bid me adieu, that I was obliged to leave the parade in a flood of tears."

144   "It will be but a"—Hamilton 17. Exactly when during his last moments Andre said this is uncertain. Prepared beforehand, it would have been saved, I'm sure, for a critical point in the proceedings, when it would produce a shattering impact, which in fact it did.

144   *Washington's absence*: Curiously intriguing for many writers is Washington's staying away from the execution, prompting any number of guesses as to why he was absent. Personally I find it to be quite a natural decision in the circumstances. He didn't attend or consult on the trial itself, never questioned or visited Andre in person, didn't hesitate to confirm the court's recommended death sentence, and used him as a pawn in the effort to get hold of Arnold. It is too easy to forget that in the fall of 1780 Washington's whole being was caught up in the minute-by-minute effort to keep the faltering Revolution alive. As compelling as the Andre story is to us today, to Washington in his time, once the plot was defeated, Andre was only one more name on a steadily lengthening list of crucial names and events. All too well Washington knew how heavy was his responsibility as commander. On the day when the last-minute negotiations over Andre between Generals Greene and Robertson were under way (October 1), Washington at his headquarters in the De Windt house was firing off letters left and right on urgent army business. Replenishing the dwindling supplies of food and other materials for the ragged troops and storing up hay and grain

for the horses prompted three letters, including one to Congress ("I do not think it will be possible, even with stripping the inhabitants entirely, to subsist the horses after the grass fails. I think it my duty to mention these matters in time, that Congress may endeavor to concert some measures for our relief before we are overtaken by winter."). Another letter that same day went to General St. Clair appointing him to the command of West Point and lengthily explaining needed defensive measures for the area. At this same time Washington even concerned himself with writing out detailed, specific directives for the spies he was sending into New York City to find if the British meant to move in force against West Point ("Get into the City . . . learn the designs of the enemy . . . whether they have any views of operating against this army, which will be best known by their preparations of waggons, horses, etc., these will want shoeing, repairing, etc. Collecting together . . . whether any troops have been imbarked and for what place," etc.). All these documents are available in Fitzpatrick 104-109. It is likely that other documents, showing Washington even busier, have been lost. Attending Andre's hanging was not something that would have loomed large on his schedule that day.

144   "Only this, gentlemen"—Hamilton 17; Thatcher 228; *Souvenir* 166 (quoting Dr. Hall, an eyewitness, as published in *Knickerbocker Magazine*, xviii, 1840, 356). So familiar, so easy-sounding is Andre's calling attention to his admittedly marvelous (of course quite deliberate) bravery at the ultimate moment that few have dared to openly question it. But only a little reflection—particularly in light of Nathan Hale's glowing testimonial to his country as the noose fell round *his* neck—uncovers its falsity. In 1876 Grenville Tremain, speaking at the dedication of the Williams monument at Schoharie, New York, said that "in comparison with the glory that surrounds . . . our own Nathan Hale, the conduct of Andre pales into a glimmering twilight" (Schoharie *Union*, September 29, 1876).

146   "The wagon was very"—Barber and Howe 77, quoted in Sargent 447. The soldier supplying the eyewitness description is identified only as "a private." Dr. Hall, regimental surgeon, remembered that Andre was "a small man, and seemed hardly to stretch the rope, and his legs dangled so much that the hangman was ordered to take hold of them and keep them straight. The body was cut down after hanging fifteen or twenty minutes." (*Centennial* 166, quoting the *Knickerbocker* 1840). The soldier

who cut the body down, William Branch, lived another seventy years, dying at the age of ninety-two (obit. Cleveland *Herald*, April 15, 1849).

146   "all the spectators"—Tallmadge 57. Same for the next quotation in this paragraph.

146   "so great that it was"—Sargent 447-48, quoting from Barber and Howe 78.

146   *Burial of Andre*: Thatcher 228; Sargent 447; Abbatt 76. Dr. Hall (*Centennial* 167) says that "from the location of the grave, Andre must have passed it in going to the place of execution." This is true, and if not actually passing it, he would certainly have noticed it. In that case, recalling the unfailing courtesy shown Andre in his captivity, I believe that the open grave would have been well covered, even disguised.

147   "The place is distinctly"—Partridge 58. That night Partridge spent at the Mabie Tavern, then still very much in business. The proprietor, Mr. Dubey, "showed me the room in which [Andre] was confined and told me it was in very nearly the same state as at the time of his confinement." Partridge measured the room and found it to be eighteen feet by twelve, with a fairly low ceiling, seven and a half feet.

148   *Exhumation of Andre:*—Buchanan's own account (*The Era*, December 1901) is quoted at length in Boylan 249-51; see also Abbatt 82-83.

148   "Excited as we were"—Boylan 249, quoting Buchanan.

148   "contained from eight"—Boylan 250. Buchanan adds that these local ladies "were loud in their praise of the prince for thus at length honoring one who still lived in their recollection with unsubdued sympathy." He does not add that many other locals were loud in condemning such sympathy for Andre as dishonoring Washington, an attitude that lingered long in the neighborhood.

148   "The laborers proceeded"—Boylan 251, quoting Buchanan.

150   "The skeleton of the brave"—New York *Courier*, August 12, 1821. The hair and the leather string found in the coffin were sent to Andre's family in Bath, England (his three sisters still lived in the family home at No. 22, the Circus, where for a time Gainsborough was a close neighbor).

151   "I descended into the"—Boylan 251, quoting Buchanan.

IX: ANDRE'S REVENGE

152   "I do not know the"—*Proceedings* 5.

153 "I now have the pleasure"—*Proceedings* 6. Same for the quotation in the next paragraph.

153 *The Congressional Resolution: Centennial* 127-28, quoting from *The Annals of Congress*, 1780.

154 *Bestowal of medals*: Roe 7; *Centennial* 148; Roscoe 465; Simms 652-53.

154 "be hunted like partridges"—Benson 64.

155 *Paulding captured and Wounded*: recorded by himself in his 1817 affidavit, *Centennial* 148; see also Roe 8. A wartime comrade of Paulding's, Abraham Boyce, later recalled his friend's "reputation for remarkable address and activity" as a soldier, and described the incident in which he was wounded. He also makes it clear that the British recognized Paulding as one of Andre's captors. In a brief action near Sing Sing early in 1783 the Westchester militia was defeated and most of the company taken:

> Paulding was making his escape over the ice when he was surrounded by several of the refugees [Tories] who commanded him to surrender. He consented to do so if they would give him quarter. They asked his name, to which he replied, "I ran as fast as I could." [Boyce means that instead of giving his name he made a break for freedom, but was run down.] They again asked his name and he made the same reply [tried to run], believing that his life would pay the forfeit of his name being known at that time, such was the hostility his exploits had excited against him on the part of the Tories. He was finally recognized by one of his captors who, closing upon him, [delivered] a severe cut with a sabre over the head, which laid him bleeding and senseless on the ice where he stood. When he recovered from the stunning effect of the blow he found himself surrounded by enemies who threatened to take his life . . . Great importance was attached to the capture of this prisoner . . . He was put in close confinement, and not long afterward peace was declared.
>
> [Meade 276 gives the whole letter. Boyce shared Paulding's earlier captivity, in New York's notorious Sugar House.]

155 "while Arnold is handed"—Hamilton 22.

156 "sprang from a heart"—Schoharie *Union*, September 29, 1876, 2.

156 "Andre left as a legacy"—*Centennial* 117. The words are those of

Chauncey Depew, speaking at the 1880 dedication of the captors monument in Tarrytown.

156 "revenge his failure by"—*Centennial* 65.

156 *Tallmadge background:* The best source for the personal life before and after the war is the biography by C. S. Hall (1943). His military service is also well-covered by Hall but needs to be supplemented by Pennypacker, Van Doren, and Tallmadge's own *Memoir.* Actually, Tallmadge is one of the overlooked Revolutionary War figures, whose military service, in particular as a pioneer intelligence officer, deserves a full-length volume of its own.

157 *Paulding background:* The amount of personal information on Paulding in print is small: see Drimmer, Roe, Browning, and Hufeland, also Constant 171-74. More is available in certain papers and documents preserved at the Field Library, Peekskill, New York. One interesting but unrecorded fact is his being a cousin of the well-known author, James Kirke Paulding. He also had a distant link to Washington Irving, whose brother William married the sister of J. K. Paulding. For sources on his son, Commodore Hiram Paulding, see Meade, *passim,* and below 221.

158 "He states that he is"—*Annals of Congress* (1817), 474. Same for the quotations from the *Annals of Congress* in the subsequent paragraphs, 474-75.

161 "has drawn down much"—New York *Evening Post,* January 16, 1817.

161 "ventured to ascribe"—New York *Courier,* January 18, 1817. Same for the next quotation from the *Courier.*

162 "received with surprise"—*Annals of Congress* (1817), 475. Same for the quotations from the *Annals* in the next paragraph.

163 "Give me leave to"—Tallmadge 134. This passage is missing from the letter as quoted by Sparks 258.

164 "Knowing the circumstances"—Tallmadge 136-37.

165 *Affidavits of Van Wart and Paulding:* Published in many newspapers at the time; see New York *Evening Post* and *National Intelligencer,* May 12, 1817, and in many sources since: see *Centennial* 143-48.

167 "I shall not further"—Garden 292-93. It is ridiculous, adds Garden, "to deprive such men of honours that not only established their fame but increased the reputation of their country, merely on the report and the suggestions of the prisoner."

167 "common highwaymen"—Boylan 210. The three, adds Boylan, were "waiting for some wealthy-looking horseman to come along in order to

mug him . . . they were interested in money, not glory or patriotism . . . didn't care about politics as much as they yearned for loot." For this damning portrait he offers neither source nor evidence, and is apparently unaware that the charges go back to Andre himself.

In an otherwise interesting article, Robert Arner, while reviewing attitudes in early American literature towards Andre's death, goes out of his way to condemn the captors. "They roamed the Neutral Ground," he writes, "in search of whatever prey turned up, and could not always be counted on to make nice distinctions between British and American sympathizers so long as there was money to be had." His sources he gives as Flexner and Abbatt, where they quote what Andre himself had to say about his supposedly avaricious captors. As with so many writers, if he was aware of the distinction at all, he never thinks to question Andre's accuracy or honesty.

A surrender, of sorts, on the point among historians is reached with the most recent full Andre biography (Hatch, 1986). There the *fact* of the disagreement is carefully reflected, avoiding any conclusion but still maintaining the original distortion, no doubt unwittingly. Comments Hatch: "Even as the versions of the capture differ, so the motive of the captors has been called in question. The three would be hailed as heroes by both Congress and the public . . . Yet both Lt. King and his senior officer, Major Tallmadge, would maintain that the three had robbery in mind while they lurked by the bridge" (245). No hint is given the reader that the opinions of King and Tallmadge were not their own, but came directly from the lips of the mortified Andre. The unfortunate impression is left that the two are relying on personal, first-hand knowledge.

169   "a rather scruffy lot"—Purcell 31; also Kail 40.

169   "one of the three"—*National Intelligencer*, February 28, 1818. The *Spectator* mention was on February 25, 1818.

169   *Tallmadge proposes widow's pension*: This fact—curiously, reported here for the first time—is recorded in *Annals of Congress* (1818), p. 1780, where the motion is attributed to "Mr. Wilkin." But the volume's detailed Index gives the initiator as Rep. Ben Tallmadge.

169   *Funerals of Paulding and Van Wart*: Peekskill *Evening Star*, October 30, 1948, in a story on the Paulding monument by City historian W. T. Horton. The story quotes from the original West Point order detailing the squad of twenty men to attend the funeral, among them Tallmadge's

son George. For his father's remark on the coincidence see Tallmadge 138. The Van Wart funeral is described in Hufeland 46; see also *Centennial* 64.

170   *David Williams at the New York festival*: New York *Evening Post*, November 24–December 4, 1830; Simms 655-66. Specifically he was a guest of the city's Ninth Ward, which sent a man all the way to Schoharie to accompany the elderly Williams down to New York City. At a grand ball in the Ninth Ward on the 30th a toast was drunk to Williams and his "incorruptible integrity" in the capture of Andre. Upon this "the venerable old gentleman involuntarily arose from his seat and burst into tears, which were mingled with those of many present" (New York *Standard*, December 1, 1830). A few minutes later Williams himself rose to offer a toast, reported by the *Evening Post* as "Our Constitution, may it ever remain what it now is, for if ever altered, the whole fabric will be defaced."

170   "the old soldier entered"—New York *Evening Post*, December 1, 1830.

171   "quite overcome with emotion"—*Evening Post*, November 29, 1830. An ad in the *Evening Post* the day of the play stated that "The celebrated David Williams, one of the captors of Andre, will be present this evening, and after the first play will relate the particulars of that interesting capture." For the gala performance the theatre generously kept to its regular price scale: box seats 75 cents, pit 37½ cents, gallery 25 cents.

171   *Death of Williams*: Soon after his return from New York City in December 1830 "he began rapidly to fail. The excitement attending his visit had no doubt been too great for one of his age and retired habits . . . At times he suffered great pains in his limbs and breast, which could only be relieved by opium as an anodyne . . . He continued gradually to waste away until sunset on Tuesday, the 2nd day of August 1831, when he expired without a struggle or a groan. The last time he spoke was on Monday morning to give some directions about the place of his burial" (Simms 656). He left one son, seven grandchildren, and his wife, who survived him by almost twenty years. His Andre pension was stopped at his death, but some time later his wife managed to have it reinstated (Simms 656; Raymond 9).

Williams's funeral also had its military salute. He was buried at Livingstonville "in the presence of a large concourse of citizens . . . at 10 o'clock a sermon was preached . . . after the sermon a procession was formed in the following order: military, Reverend clergy, Pall Bearers, relatives, and citizens. At the grave an appropriate eulogy was pronounced by R. McClellan Esq., and the farewell salute of the military closed the exercises" (Simms 657, quoting a local newspaper account). The transferral of the remains in 1876 to the Old Stone Fort, Schoharie, left a good deal of lingering resentment in Livingstonville.

EPILOGUE: LOOSE ENDS

173 *The four monuments:* Paulding—W. Horton in Peekskill *Evening Star,* October 30, 1948; Williams—Schoharie *Union,* September 29, 1876; Van Wart—Benson 133, Hufeland 46; the Captors—*Centennial* 8-25; for the 1880 addition see *Centennial* 69-81.

175 "help us so to live"—Reverend Van Wart's whole prayer, a lengthy one, is quoted in *Centennial* 89-91.

175 *Award to Andre's family:* Sargent 457-58, Sparks 307-09. Andre's brother was also a soldier, a captain in the Twenty-sixth Foot. The baronetcy was conferred on William "and his male heirs forever." It lasted only to 1802, when William's male line failed.

176 *The Seward monody:* Well-liked in its day as expressing the resentment of Britons on the death of Andre, its 460 lines have little true poetry in them but much swollen rhetoric and overwrought sentiment. Variously published, it is now most accessible in the reprint of the Joshua Smith *Narrative.*

177 *Attempt to kidnap Arnold:* The facts about Sargent Champe and his mission became known very early and the story has been told many times since. For a full account see Bakeless 302-17; also Randall 578-79, and *William and Mary Quarterly,* 1939-40, 322-42, 548-55.

178 "I will here request"—J. H. Smith 33. The fullest treatment of Smith, his involvement in the plot, and his trial is in the biography by Richard Koke. In reality, concludes Koke, Smith was nothing more than "an obscure dupe" in the treason plot, tricked by the wily Arnold into believing that he was somehow aiding the American cause: "the misfortune that overtook him and branded him a shady character—even a traitor—is typical of the tragedies of war" (249). Maybe. But my own reading of the evidence gives Smith more credit than that for intelligence. In Smith's position during those clandestine hours only an imbecile would have failed to suspect *something,* especially if he saw Arnold pass papers to the British officer (that point remains uncertain).

I believe that Smith did not have full knowledge of the plot, but mainly because he *chose* not to know, and Arnold was content that he shouldn't know. I'm convinced, further, that the notion of surrendering West Point to the British never occurred to him—which leaves the question: what then *did* he think was going on?

179   *Admiral Hiram Paulding*: The 1910 biography by his daughter, Rebecca Meade, is a sympathetic portrait, but full and detailed. For a summary of his long naval career see Hammersley 21-22; for the Nicaraguan intervention see Carr 233-39, and Meade 180-200, 278-85. As an eighteen-year-old midshipman Hiram saw action on Lake Champlain in the War of 1812 and in 1816 served under Decatur in the action against Algiers. In 1826 he spent almost a year chasing a mob of mutineers across the Pacific. In 1830 in searching for information about his father he wrote one of his father's old comrades, Abraham Boyce, prompting a long reply which preserves much detail about John Paulding's war service (Meade 274-77).

181   *Remarks of Rep. Haskin*: These are quoted from a contemporary pamphlet publication of the entire speech, delivered on January 5 "in defense of Commodore Hiram Paulding." (Copy kindly supplied by the Field Library, Peekskill, New York.)

183   "By far the greatest"—Quoted in Biddle 413. The whole nine-page section on Andre from Mahon is printed in Biddle 404-413.

183   ". . . it must be borne"—Quoted in Biddle 411.

184   "When Andre was arrested"—Quoted in Biddle 412.

185   "All laws which are not"—Anon., *North American Review*, 256.

185   "a new light"—Haines 31; for the new theory see 35-36.

186   *Discovery of Andre's diary*: New York *Times*, March 31, 1901 reports the finding of the diary among the possessions of Lord Grey of London, great-grandson of General Charles Grey, "who commanded British troops in the Revolution." The diary has been published several times and is now most accessible in the Arno Press reprint.

186   "unable to form"—Sargent 122.

186   "Grey so skilfully led"—Sargent 220. Sargent attempts further paliation of Andre's role in the massacre by suggesting that he was the unidentified captain who spared those Americans surrendering to him. But this unknown captain was an officer of the Second Light Infantry, while Andre was Grey's aide-de-camp (see Demarest 43).

186   "greatly censured in our"—Sargent 221. In a footnote to this curiously

noncommittal statement, Sargent adds that "I am inclined to think that Andre celebrated these and other feats of the light infantry in appropriate verse" but says he can't be sure of the authorship of the compositions he has in mind, referring to several British publications. His styling as "feats" of British soldiery the massacres at Paoli and Old Tappan is strange, to say the least.

186   "Andre heard steel"—Flexner 155.

187   "put to the bayonet"—New York *Gazette and Mercury*, December 1, 1778, quoted in Flexner 155, also in the Andre *Diary* 95.

187   *Baylor massacre burials*: The six bodies had been dumped into tanning vats. One of the skulls showed a large fracture at the side, the bone being "punched into the cranial cavity." Experiment showed that the wound had been made by the butt of a musket while the victim was lying prostrate, "with his head turned to his right . . . he was probably bayoneted first and then killed with the musket's butt" (Mazur, *Excavation Report* 22-23). Eventually one of the six was identified as Sergeant Isaac Davenport, of Dorchester, Massachusetts, aged twenty-six. A very full account of the discovery, the excavation, and the massacre itself is in Thomas Demarest's article in *Bergen County History*. It quotes the original documents—letters, depositions, etc.—resulting from a congressional investigation of the shameful incident, which was well and indignantly noticed in newspapers at the time.

At the time of the 1967 discovery this author was living in the area and visited the excavation site many times. It is one thing to read descriptions of the massacre, to hear Andre coolly telling how Grey's marauding troops "stabbed great numbers" of the helpless Americans. It is quite another to stand at the side of the deepening pit and watch as the bones of the long-dead men slowly appear from under the dark soil.

SELECTED BIBLIOGRAPHY

Listed here are all the printed works named or referred to in the text and Notes, along with a number of items that provided general background on Andre, his captors, the Revolution, and West Point.

Anon., "An Authentic Account of Major Andre's Death," *Political Magazine* (London), II, 1781, 171-73.

———, "Lord Mahon's Last Volume," *North American Review*, January 1855, 247-57.

———, "Minutes of a Court of Inquiry Upon the Case of Major John Andre" (pamphlet), Albany, 1865.

———, "Major Andre's Monument," New York *Times*, October 3, 4, 20, 22, 1879.

———, "Where Was Andre Buried?" New York *World*, August 30, September 8, 14-15, 21-23, 29, October 7, 12, 1879.

———, "Bibliographic Notes on Poems and Ballads Relating to Major Andre," *Magazine of American History*, August 1892, 217-20.

———, *The Old Dutch Burial Ground of Sleepy Hollow* (pamphlet), Historical Society of Tappan Zee, 1926.

Abbatt, W., *The Crisis of the Revolution, Being the Story of Arnold and Andre*, (1899), repr. Harbor Hill Books, 1976.

Andre, J., *Major Andre's Journal: Operations of the British Army, June 1777 to November 1778*, Tarrytown, N.Y., 1930.

Arner, R., "The Death of Major Andre: Some 18th Century Views," *Early American Literature* XI, No. 1, Spring 1976.

Bacon, E., "The Capture of Andre," *Bulletin of the Westchester County Historical Society*, April 1930.

Bakeless, J., *Turncoats, Traitors, and Heroes*, Lippincott, 1959.

Baldwin, J., "The Disinterment of Major Andre," *The Era*, December 1901.

Benson, E., *Vindication of the Captors of Major Andre* (1817), repr. New York, 1865.

Biddle, C., "The Case of Major Andre," *Memoirs of the Historical Society of Pennsylvania* VI, 1858, 319-416.

Bilias, G., *George Washington's Generals*, Morrow, 1964.

Bolton, R., *History of Westchester County*, New York, 1848.

Boylan, B., *Benedict Arnold: The Dark Eagle*, Norton, 1981.

Brown, R., "Three Forgotten Heroes," *American Heritage*, May 1957.

Campbell, C., "Smith's House At Haverstraw, New York," *Magazine of American History*, July 1890.

Canning J., and Buxton, W., *History of the Tarrytowns*, Harbor Hill Books, 1975.

Carr, A., *The World of William Walker*, Harper's, 1963.

Centennial Souvenir of the Monument Association of the Capture of Major Andre, N. C. Husted, ed., Tarrytown, 1880.

Clinton, Sir H., *The American Rebellion*, London 1954.

Constant, Rev. S., *Journal*, Lippincott, 1903.

Dann, J., *The Revolution Remembered*, Chicago, 1980.

Davis, B., *George Washington and the American Revolution*, Random House, 1975.

Dawson, H., *Record of the Trail of Joshua H. Smith*, New York, 1866.

Decker, M., *Ten Days of Infamy*, Arno Press, 1969.

Demarest, T., "The Baylor Massacre," *Bergen County History*, 1971 Annual, 21-93.

Drimmer, H., "Major Andre's Captors: The Changing Perspective of History," *Westchester Historian* V, 75, Spring 1999.

Dykman, J., "The Last Twelve Days of Major Andre," *Magazine of American History*, May-July 1889.

Egleston, T., *Life of John Paterson, Major-General in the Revolutionary Army*, Putnam, 1898.

Fitzpatrick, J., *The Writings of George Washington*, Vol. XX, Washington, D.C., 1931-44.

Flexner, J., *The Traitor and the Spy*, Little, Brown, 1953, 1975.

Freeman, D., *George Washington, A Biography*, Scribner's, 1951.

Garden, A., *Anecdotes of the Revolutionary War in America*, Charleston, 1822.

Greene, G., *Life of Nathanael Greene, Major-General in the Revolution* (1871), repr. Newport, N.Y., 1972.

Greene, N., *The Papers of General Nathanael Greene*, D. Conrad, ed., Univ. of North Carolina, 1991.

Haines, H., "The Execution of Major Andre," *English Historical Review* V, 1890.

Hall, C., *Benjamin Tallmadge: Revolutionary Soldier and American Businessman*, Columbia Univ. Press, 1943.

Hamilton, A., *The Fate of Major Andre* (pamphlet), New York, 1916.,

Hammersley, L., *Records of the Living Officers of the U.S. Navy and Marine Corps*, Philadelphia, 1878.

Haskin, J., *Remarks in Defense of Commodore Hiram Paulding*, Washington, D.C. (pamphlet, House of Reps), 1856.

Hatch, R., *Major John Andre: A Gallant in Spy's Clothing*, Houghton, 1986.

Headley, P., *Life of LaFayette*, New York, 1847.

Hendrickson, R., *Alexander Hamilton*, New York, 1976.

Holmes, L., *David Williams and the Capture of Major Andre* (pamphlet), Mohawk Valley History Assoc., Schenectady, 1926.

Hufeland, O., "The Capture of Major Andre," in *Westchester County During the American Revolution*, Tarrytown, 1926.

Idzerda, S., *LaFayette and the Age of the American Revolution*, Cornell Univ., 1980.

Irving, W., *The Life of Washington*, Vols. 2,4, Putnam, 1861.

Kail, J., *Who Was Who During the Revolution*, Indianapolis, 1976.

Koke, R., *Accomplice in Treason: Joshua Hett Smith and the Arnold Conspiracy*, New York Historical Society, 1973.

LaFayette, the Marquis de, *Memoirs*, London, 1837.

Leake, I., *Life of Col. Lamb*, Albany, 1850.

Lomask, M., "Benedict Arnold: The Aftermath of Treason," *American Heritage*, October 1967.

Lossing, B., *Pictorial Field Book of the Revolution*, New York, 1851.

———, *The Two Spies*, New York, 1886.

Mazur, B., and Daniels, W., *Baylor's Dragoons Massacre Excavation Report*, 1978 (Pamphlet, 24 pp.).

McCracken, H., "Andre: A Case of Modern Folklore," *New York Folklore Quarterly* XV, 1927.

Meade, R., *Life of Hiram Paulding, Rear-Admiral U.S.N.*, Baker and Taylor, 1910.

Meehan, J., "Major Andre and Bath," in *More Famous Houses of Bath and District*, Bath, 1906.

Morse, J., *Life of Alexander Hamilton*, New York, 1876.

Palmer, D., *The River and the Rock: A History of West Point*, Greenwood Press, 1969.

Partridge, A., "Andre's Grave At Tappan," *Magazine of American History* V, 1880.

Pennypacker, M., *General Washington's Spies*, New York, 1939.

Proceedings of A Board of General Officers Held By Order of His Excellency Gen. Washington . . . Respecting Major John Andre. Printed by order of the U.S. Congress, Philadelphia, 1780.

Purcell, E., *Who Was Who in the Revolution*, New York, 1993.

Randall, W., *Benedict Arnold: Patriot and Traitor*, Morrow, 1990.

Raymond, M., *David Williams and the Capture of Major Andre* (pamphlet), Tarrytown, 1903.

Roe, C., "Andre's Captors: A Study In Values," *Westchester Historian*, Fall 1966; repr. *York State Tradition*, Winter 1967.

———, *Major Andre's Watches*, Tarrytown, 1971.

Roscoe, H., *History of Schoharie County* (New York), Albany, 1926.

Sargent, W., "John Andre and Honora Sneyd," *Atlantic Monthly*, December 1860.

———, *The Life and Career of Major John Andre*, New York, 1861.

Scharf, T., *History of Westchester County* (New York), 2 vols., Philadelphia, 1886.

Simms, J., *History of Schoharie County and Border Wars of New York*, Albany, 1948.

Smith, H., *Andreana*, New York, 1865.

Smith, J. H., *An Authentic Narrative of the Causes which Led to the Death of Major Andre*, London, 1808, repr. New York, 1931.

Sparks, J., *Life of Washington*, New York, 1838.

———, *Life and Treason of Benedict Arnold*, New York, 1835.

Stevens, J., "The DeWindt House at Tappan, N.Y., Washington's Headquarters," *Magazine of American History*, V. 5, 1880.

Tallmadge, B., [His speech in Congress regarding Andre's captors], *Annals of Congress*, 1817, 474-75; see also 1137-38, 1779-82.

————, *Memoir of Col. Benjamin Tallmadge, Prepared by Himself at the Request of His Children*, Society of the Sons of the Revolution of New York State, 1858, repr. with Notes, New York, 1904.

Thane, E., *The Fighting Quaker, Nathanael Greene*, New York, 1972.

Thatcher, J., *Military Journal of the American Revolution*, New York, 1862.

Tillotson, H., *The Beloved Spy, The Life and Loves of Major Andre*, Caldwell, Idaho, 1948.

Van Doren, C., *Secret History of the American Revolution*, New York, 1941.

Wallace, W., *Traitorous Hero: The Life and Fortunes of Benedict Arnold*, New York, 1954.

Waln, R., *The Life of LaFayette*, New York, 1825.

Webb, J., *Reminiscences of General Samuel Webb*, New York, 1882.

Webb, S., *Correspondence and Journals of Samuel B. Webb*, 3 vols., New York, 1893.

Wilcox, C., "The Ethics of Andre's Mission," a talk given before the New York State Historical Society, 1915, repr. in Andre's *Journal*, see above.

Wilcox, W., *Portrait of a General: Sir Henry Clinton in the War of Independence*, New York, 1964.

Wilson, L., "Andre's Landing Place at Haverstraw: A Mooted Question Settled," *Magazine of American History* XIII, 1885.

————, "Andre and His Landing Place," *Magazine of American History*, February 1910.

ACKNOWLEDGEMENTS

The first debt of any writer who deals with a controverted, two-centuries-old figure or event is always to those scholars and other investigators who preceded him. With Andre there have been quite a lot, and I herewith tender them one and all my sincerest thanks for their work in preserving materials, for stimulating discussion, and for their help generally in clearing the ground. Their names may be read in my Notes and Bibliography.

More particularly my thanks go to the graciously accommodating staffs of various libraries: The University of Wisconsin Memorial and Historical Libraries, Madison; The Public Library, Old-Tappan, New York; The Field Library, Peekskill, New York; The Dixon Homestead Library, Dumont, New Jersey; the Public Library and Captors' Museum, Tarrytown, New York; Library of the Schoharie County (New York) Historical Society; New York Public Library; Library of the U.S. Naval Academy, Annapolis; library of the U.S. Military Academy, West Point.

My particular gratitude goes also to my sons John, Tim, and Matt for their informed company on our several visits to the Andre sites and for their careful readings of the manuscript. As always, for her understanding my thanks go to my patient wife Dorothy.

INDEX

Italic page references signify illustrations.